ARRIS ILLUSTRATED

Contents

MAO
AND THE CHINESE REVOLUTION

MAO'S
REVOLUTIONS

THE HISTORY OF CONTEMPORARY CHINA IS INSEPARABLE FROM THE RISE OF MAO. INVENTOR OF HIS OWN BRAND OF COMMUNISM, BOTH TYRANT AND PERPETUAL REBEL, HE IS THE FATHER OF THE TRAGIC UTOPIA THAT WAS MAOISM.

In spite of de-Maoization and the reforms undertaken by his unfaithful successor, Deng Xiaoping, Mao Zedong (1893–1976) remains an exceptional figure in a century replete with revolutionaries, founders of empires, and totalitarian dictators. Mao's unique position comes from being all three at once: the burning soul of a revolution that he dominated after a long struggle, the patriarch of a country he transformed into a powerful nation, the commander of a people that he spurred on beyond human limits, until his dying breath.

In 1912, following the fall of the Qing dynasty (conquerors from Manchuria in power since 1644), Mao joined Sun Yat-sen's republican army. In 1921, almost by chance, he was one of the thirteen founders of the Chinese Communist Party. But it was no longer chance that found him, after Chiang Kai-shek's brutal crushing of urban communists in 1921, a guerrilla. He became the leader of the Long March (1934–35), leader of communist resistance to the Japanese occupation (1937–1945), and finally, leader of the victorious side in the Civil War against the Guomindang. With the People's Republic proclaimed on October 1st, 1949, one would think the revolution over; on the contrary. Collectivization in 1955, the Great Leap Forward in 1958–59, and the Cultural Revolution ten years later, all accelerated Mao's drive toward his distinct brand of socialism, with a shortcut via communism, and his elimination of the bourgeoisie. These upheavals steadily turned the people against

The Chinese people have recovered from the illusions and the terrors of Maoism. But the perennial image of the man who was, for better or for worse, the dominant figure of their history remains prominent, here seen over the arch leading to the tribune of Tiananmen, gateway to the Forbidden City of the Emperors.
Ph. © Burri/Magnum

him, including his most loyal allies, Liu Shaoqi and Deng Xiaoping, who would become architect of the dismantling of the Maoist system after 1978.

Mao, born with the rise of nationalism and the revolutionary movement, died as the revolution ended. His dates more accurately coincide with those of the revolution than those of Sun Yat-sen (1866–1925), who died before the first soviets and the Long March, or Deng Xiaoping (born in 1904), who was too young to have taken up arms against the last emperor. Of course, it is his system, Maoism, more than his biography, which made him into the symbol of the Chinese Revolution.

This "Chinese Way" toward socialism, which set Mao apart from Lenin and Marx, was rooted in the specific traits of a crisis dating back to the 18th century, before Japanese and Western incursions initiated the process that would make China into the prototypical third world country. Guerrilla warfare in the countryside during the thirties, anti-Japanese nationalism after the 1937 invasion, anti-Americanism and the break with the soviets at the end of the fifties were all factors that contributed to the true third world communist revolutionary that was Mao.

True, Stalin was no less a nationalist, with his "socialism in one country" and the holy Russian crusade against Hitler. But nationalism had no part in the Bolsheviks' strategy in 1917; nor was there any mobilization of the rural masses. Economic distress and the mistakes of other parties were to deliver them to the communists, when the moment was ripe. A risky venture, for though peasants had revolted during the chaos of 1917, they remained a taboo subject for the new regime, which had to make considerable efforts in their direction while creating a socialist state. In China, however, the communist party apparatus was in place well before 1949 in rural areas; indeed, its influence in these zones of guerrilla warfare was an integral part of its rise to national power.

The Dowager Empress Cixi (1835–1908). An explosive mix of cruelty and seduction, with a highly-developed political intelligence, Cixi oscillated between reformers and conservatives, thus maintaining her position until the end of the Empire. Not unlike Deng Xiaoping, whom historians often compare to her.
Ph © M. Durazzo/ANA

The authoritarian aspects of the Leninist-Stalinist model were certainly present in Maoism: the avant-garde imposed its will on the people in the name of the "dictatorship of the proletariat," and soon became a rigid, totalitarian bureaucracy. From the 1940s, the Party behaved as a state, aiming to dominate society through revolutionary mobilization. Today, this observation seems unremarkable, but we forget how de-Maoization, the demise of European communism and the collapse of the Soviet Union have made Mao and Maoism far removed today. Criticism and history itself have driven a wedge between us and the communist myth; the "Great Red Sun" has finally set. But it wasn't so easy to speak frankly about Maoist China 20 or 30 years ago, when Mao was idolized by a good portion of the left-leaning intelligentsia in Europe. One didn't say China, but the "Chinese model." Mao redeemed the sins of Stalin—for everyone except the die-hard Stalinists. Even thinkers to the right of center thought Mao the best excuse for Maoism, for was he not hostile to the Soviet Union? Was his "model" not radically different from the Soviet one? These people turned a blind eye to the fact that his regime was every bit as totalitarian, and instead saw in Mao the savior of an orphan nation, "scattered like sand," as Sun Yat-sen had said, after the fall of the Emperor.

So called progressives admired Mao's "permanent revolution," which was supposed to prevent the exercise of power from becoming a mere routine. Unlike Trotsky, the "disarmed prophet" planned to accelerate the transition to socialism by developing the class struggles born of pre-Revolutionary society. Mao considered the two units—society and the Party—inseparable, melded together in the revolutionary crucible and perpetually kept "active"; in other words, mobilized, indoctrinated, and corrected constantly. This unrest could be directed either toward external enemies (Japan, the US, the USSR, the bourgeoisie, landowners), or toward those evils that Mao knew were

Dr. Sun Yat-sen, M.D., President of the Republic (1912), founder of the Guomindang, ally of the CCP (1923) although an anti-communist theoretician who defended the Three Principles, was above all the apostle of China's opening up to the modern world, as a sovereign nation and in keeping with traditions he considered useful. It is not surprising that his prestige has never been higher, from Beijing to Taiwan... Ph © Coll. Viollet

The danger of a restoration of capitalism exists in China. If we forget the class struggle […], a socialist country such as ours will become its own opposite, degenerating into capitalism.

Mao Zedong,

September 1962

unavoidable: the inertia of the masses, intellectual deviations, bureaucratization, and the party cadres, who themselves became bourgeois. Actually, Mao transformed into a crucial strength the fundamental handicap of his undertaking: the closed, unpoliticized peasantry in which it was born. But in politicizing Chinese society and the Party, Mao dominated them utterly, and substituted a totalitarian system for the anarchy that could have resulted. After the rural guerrilla struggles and the Long March, Mao wreaked havoc as unforgiving master of the peasantry, terror of the intellectuals, and butcher of the Red Guards.

This intense activism aimed to transcend objective limits to development (lack of capital, overpopulation, etc.) through the mobilization of the work force and the creation of a new humanity, selfless and free of material obsession. Mao as anti-Stalin, as super-democrat, as super-Prometheus, dreamed of giving communism back its original vocation, left by the wayside in Prague, Budapest, and Moscow: that of totally emancipating mankind. This omnipotent vision only aggravated the liabilities of the regime. Prometheus allowed himself to be worshipped, the country to be starved, and the double bind of anarchy and bureaucracy to defeat his aims of development for China. When the army quelled the Red Guard uprising in 1968, China had become a fully-fledged third world country, with no resemblance to the sublime image fashionably entertained in some quarters of the West. Maoism was utopia turned nightmare: despotism barely hidden beneath the

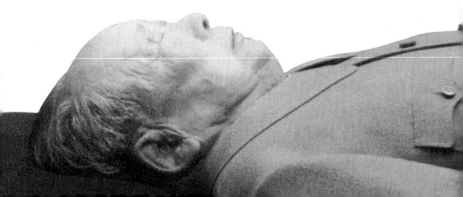

smooth smile of its prophet, police tyranny calling itself political mobilization, with the corruption and privileges of the nomenklatura impervious to the militant rhetoric targeting these happy few, and economic and social stagnation of the masses due to the frugal egalitarianism of Mao's new Sparta.

Although the "Chinese way" has proved a failure, although Mao made mistakes as bloody and as costly as those of Stalin, rendering futile the countless discussions of the differences between the two systems and underlining the inherent banality of totalitarianism, it remains that Mao led his country on a unique path of revolution, intimately linked to the recent history of China. Since the opium wars of 1840–60, the coastal areas had benefited from economic growth and social progress, but the rest of China lagged behind. There were thus two Chinas, which the urban revolution and an initial foray into soviet style communism in the 1920s had failed to reconcile. The key to understanding 20th century China lies in this opposition between an introverted "Yellow" China, with its traditions, both agrarian and bureaucratic, and the ill-fated, Western-oriented, "Blue" China, whose birth and decline spanned the forty years from 1890 to 1930. The island of Taiwan's evolution toward modernity and democracy is indicative of what could have taken place in China had Mao not crushed its initial manifestations on the continent. Surely Deng Xiaoping had a sense of this when "modernizing" China.

The Revolution does not explain 20th-century China,

"**W**e will never do to Mao what Khrushchev did to Stalin." The architect of de-Maoization during the late seventies, Deng Xiaoping actually went much further than the Soviet leader. In the case of China, however, there was no "good" Lenin to redeem the "bad" Stalin. Mao Zedong was therefore graded: 70 percent good, 30 percent bad. His embalmed remains share a mausoleum with those of his companions, the two most prominent of whom were Liu Shaoqi and Zhou Enlai, who had been with Mao since the founding epoch of the 1940s.
Ph © Grabet/Gamma

any more than Mao represents the Revolution alone. The tiny group of intellectuals that spurred the huge rural population to espouse Mao's ideals was educated in a more open China. Maoism and the Revolution owe much to this urban culture, and so does Mao himself. Mao, the provincial schoolteacher, owed his introduction to politics and social dynamics to the cosmopolitan intellectuals who made up the first generation of Chinese communists who looked down

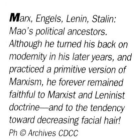

Marx, Engels, Lenin, Stalin: Mao's political ancestors. Although he turned his back on modernity in his later years, and practiced a primitive version of Marxism, he forever remained faithful to Marxist and Leninist doctrine—and to the tendency toward decreasing facial hair! Ph © Archives CDCC

馬　克　思
中国杭州织锦厂制 9.5×14.5 2 9

恩　格　斯
中国杭州织锦厂制 9.5×14.5 2 9

upon him from on high in Shanghai and Peking.

The young Mao and his contemporaries used the new urban society to revive 19th-century traditions of rebellion and activism. They succeeded in exploiting the urban society's energy and its impatience with regimes that had shown their weakness during the national crisis of the 1900s (when China was first faced with an exhausted Empire proposing timorous and tardy reforms and then, a few years later, with a budding Republic buckling under the pressure of the warlords) by tapping into its desire to take part in the rehabilitation and modernization of the country. But this prosperous, urban China stayed within its invisible borders. The winds of change hadn't reached the rest of the country, much less fanned the flames of revolution. Up until the 1930s, when worldwide depression put a lid on urban enthusiasm, and forced the communists to retreat into a countryside busy with its own crisis, development was halted by grinding poverty and the all-powerful landed gentry, rampant militarism, and the Japanese invasion of 1937.

Mao seized upon this improbable opportunity. In the 1920s his career took off when he decided to confront the crisis in China from its most marginalized, underdeveloped areas. To be sure, he did not create

列　寧

中国杭州织锦厂制 9.5×14.8公分

斯　大　林

中国杭州织锦厂制 9.5×14.8公分

毛　澤　東

中国杭州东方红丝织厂 9.5×14.8公分

the rural revolution overnight. Urban communism fell from prominence in 1927; Mao would not take up the reins of the Party until after the Long March of 1935, and his hold on it wouldn't go unchallenged until the 1940s. Nor was he the inventor of this rural strategy. Other pioneers broke the taboo when he was still reciting the Communist Manifesto's mantra of the bourgeoisie and the proletariat. And of course, guerrilla warfare had existed for a thousand years. Mao was a latecomer, not at all the inspired genius of the official portraits. It took time for circumstances to evolve in a way favorable to him, and for him to develop in a way favorable to the rural revolution.

Mao's biggest task would be to control the transition from revolution to revolutionary government, and reconcile the rebellious urges of the

Successive revolutionary episodes fashioned Mao Zedong before he left his own mark during the communist period of Yanan (1936–1945). During this time, Mao lived out his double nature of rebel and emperor for the first time, and became the uncontested leader of the Party.
Ph © Wu Yinxian/Magnum

people with the foundation of an empire during the 1940s at Yanan. He would accomplish what Chiang Kai-shek (1887–1975) and other party rivals attempted in vain, by mobilizing the masses and the Party. Nothing short of bringing China back from the depths of crisis, indeed, at a time when both the nation and the Party were in mortal danger, can be credited to a man today relegated to the purgatory of history. Was he right to transform a unique situation into a system destined to force history in a new direction? This was the vital question, for the millions of victims following 1949, and for Mao himself, who lived his life around it.

The years until 1935 were ones of apprenticeship and failures, as Mao searched for the synthesis of activism and politics that he would find in the war-torn countryside. Then, from 1936–1945, Mao grew into his authority, until he became the uncontested leader in 1945. Mao used the next ten years to bring the country under his control. After 1955, things would go sour, with Mao trying in vain to breathe new life into the socialist project, bogged down by dissenting voices within the Party, the fattening of the regime and the people's enduring poverty. Tyranny would hardly convince a weary people that utopia was just around the corner—China had lost hope in Mao.

From rebel within an Empire to rebellious emperor, Mao and his paradoxical reign are inextricably linked to his hasty synthesis of conflicting traditions. The confrontation with the West reflects this, for Maoism provoked, without resolving, enormous tensions among the intellectuals of his day. What "made" Mao was a unique relationship between an ancient order of things and the blocked energies of modernity. But how are we to choose which of these traditions, or which of the attempts at adapting them, can account for a brand of totalitarianism that belongs unequivocally in the 20th century? Understanding a China between two worlds, and a country bumpkin between two Chinas, can help to explain the strange mix of youth and senility, the sheer dizzy power that was Maoism. History surpasses psychology in its portrait of the rebel-dictator. For was it not the clash of the Great Empire and the industrialized West that, along with a few distorted traditions, put Mao in a position to proclaim himself the equal of the gods?

After the Great Leap Forward, and its 15 to 30 million victims, the Cultural Revolution was responsible, directly or indirectly, for the deaths of 100 million people—a figure that is only an official estimate. The ultimate toll of this decentralized terror planned by Mao himself, will never be known.
Ph © Roger Pic

Chapter 1

CHINA **B**ETWEEN
TWO **W**ORLDS

AFTER A CENTURY OF PEACE AND GROWTH, CHINA OPENED UP TO THE WEST IN THE 19TH CENTURY. A CRISIS ENSUED: THE ANCIENT EMPIRE FAILED TO ADAPT TO THE MODERN WORLD, AND INSTEAD COLLAPSED IN 1912.

The tension between tradition and modernity that forms the context of Maoism is a product of the 18th and 19th centuries. Chinese history has a reputation for immobility. Hegel called it "a majestically repeating ruin." For Marx, China was caught in the "jaws of time." This is pure illusion. Beyond the rituals of a seemingly immutable Confucianism, the last two centuries of the Empire were a period of exceptional evolution, though these changes ultimately led to crisis. When Westerners arrived in the mid-19th century, China had already missed out on the Industrial Revolution, and was already embarked on what is known as the descending phase of a dynastic cycle—characterized by economic distress, a disorganized administration, uprisings, and intellectual uncertainty. This turmoil weakened the Empire, but also initiated changes whose influences were to combine with those of the West.

A street in Beijing at the beginning of the 20th century. "Opened" fifty years previously, China was evolving... while remaining true to itself. Contact with the West was more conflictual than in Japan, also abruptly "opened," but more quick to undertake radical adaptations. In China, radicalism was the province of revolutionaries and intellectuals far more than of rulers. Among these, partisans of rejection were dominant until the end of the 19th century. Society itself, at least in the cities, adroitly maintained an equal distance from the two extremes.
Ph © Coll. Albert Kahn

An Evolving Empire

During the 18th century, China was on par with Europe, admired for its fine merchandise—silks, Nankin cloth, porcelain, and tea. Exports vastly exceeded imports, and Canton, the center of trade, brought wealth to the whole country. With 150 million people at the end of the 17th century (during Louis XIV's reign, France, at the time a European giant, boasted 20 million subjects), China's population doubled during the next century. The prosperous and peaceful "Middle

Kingdom," confident in its extraordinary demographic advantage and social and intellectual prestige, could haughtily reject trade offers from British ambassadors. Self-sufficiency and self-absorption coexisted in a delicate balance.

But in a growing, 18th-century China, fragility was not apparent. The manorial system, with its huge domains cultivated by serfs, prevalent throughout the Ming dynasty (1368–1644), was a thing of the past. Farmers or small landlords, even peasants were allowed to compete in national exams that opened the doors to mandarin status. Not all were able to exercise this freedom, given the length and cost of such studies. But thanks to strong community bonds, starting with the solidarity of one's own clan, many took advantage of the meritocracy. Those who stayed put were not lacking for supplementary income, either as artisans or

merchants, feeding off of the trade currents of the Empire's regional economy.

Pre-industrial growth was also changing the structure of China's cities. Local affairs were increasingly managed by the guilds, just as they were by the village notables in the countryside. For the bureaucracy, urban society was a force to be contended with, all the more so that many village notables were gravitating toward the cities, and cementing ties with the learned mandarins through business or marriage. The urban upper class gained from merchants' admission to official status (through sales of land, matrimonial alliance, or success at the mandarin exams), and the general prestige of this new urban elite in the most developed cities was considerable. Meanwhile, in the rural areas, a similar upper class was becoming more powerful, though as a looser and somewhat less

Two worlds juxtaposed without real contact: official China and the West, whose methods of government were only adopted early in the 20th century. Here, a view of the Wall of Beijing at that time; it was razed during the Great Leap Forward (1958). Ph © M. Durazzo/ANA

prestigious aggregate of landowners, administrators, accountants, tax collectors, schoolteachers, and even uneducated government clerks with no status at all.

The new social order bore little resemblance to the rigidly codified caste system (where one was either a mandarin, a peasant, an artisan, or a merchant), or for that matter to the Confucian way of conceiving society. This put the landed gentry, with access to mandarin status and the bureaucracy through the examination system, on one side, and the rest of the people on the other, as an undifferentiated mass of non-privileged, illiterate subjects.

While the growing trade economy tended to increase literacy, the Qing dynasty chose to co-manage the Empire with the notables rather than its own civil servants. A lean bureaucracy was the order of the day: only 20,000 at the end of the 19th century. During the

18th century, taxation had been modest and stable, but now local administrators had to make ends meet by inventing new taxes. They also had to pay their own assistants, often unqualified or corrupt; poor administration was often the result.

On the whole, there was very little unrest in 18th-century China. Politics was off limits to the notables, who were quite content with initiatives based on local management or philanthropy—the opposite of a politicization of a civil society organized on a national scale, independently of the State and against it. The merchants were busy attaining the next level of status, emulating the mandarins' lifestyle and culture. A fluid, yet stable Confucianism: the authorities had complete and ultimate control, and the government alone decided on the attribution of mandarin status through the exam system.

During the 19th century, this equilibrium would fall apart. Population growth, long both cause and consequence of economic growth, finally exceeded the capacities of the land and the work that people could put into it. In the fifty years from 1800 to 1850, China's population of 300 million increased by over 100 million.

Far from being the "imperialist wart" vituperated by the Maoists, China's opening up was the result of a steady evolution of "Blue" China, i.e. the urban and coastal regions, in contrast to "Yellow" China's rural inland, and its continental and agrarian worldview.

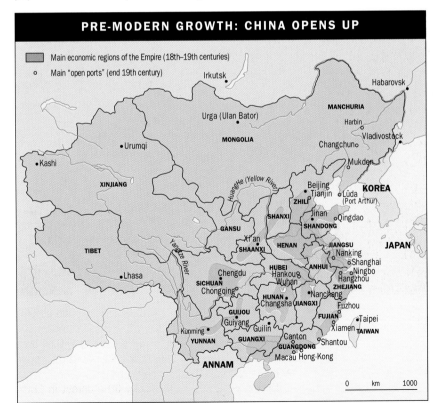

PRE-MODERN GROWTH: CHINA OPENS UP

Main economic regions of the Empire (18th–19th centuries)

Main "open ports" (end 19th century)

Irkutsk

Habarovsk

MANCHURIA

Urga (Ulan Bator)

Harbin

MONGOLIA

Vladivostock

Urumqi

Changchun

Kashi

Mukden

XINJIANG

Huanghe (Yellow River)

Beijing

KOREA

Tianjin

Lüda (Port Arthur)

ZHILI

SHANXI

Jinan

Qingdao

GANSU

SHANDONG

Xi'an

HENAN

JIANGSU

JAPAN

SHAANXI

Nanking

TIBET

Yangtze River

Shanghai

HUBEI

ANHUI

Ningbo

Lhasa

Chengdu

Hankou

Hangzhou

SICHUAN

Wuhan

ZHEJIANG

Chongqing

HUNAN

Nanchang

Changsha

JIANGXI

Fuzhou

GUIZHOU

FUJIAN

Guiyang

Taipei

Kunming

Guilin

Xiamen

TAIWAN

YUNNAN

GUANGXI

Canton

GUANGDONG

Shantou

Macau Hong-Kong

ANNAM

0   km   1000

Illegal imports of opium touched off a monetary and commercial crisis that shook the whole country, especially in the south. The mandarins were well aware of many other disruptive phenomena: people leaving the cities for the less-populated mountainous areas, deforestation, penury, famine, and increased mortality, generally from a number of causes. This massive instability made many fear a catastrophe, like Malthus in Europe, who saw a link between overpopulation, poverty, and war. However, Europe had the Industrial Revolution; China did not.

The effects of the population explosion were also felt in the spheres of power. The administrative machine was a mosaic of special interests: positions were distributed through co-optation and nepotism, and embezzlement was rampant. Neglect of public works ensued, hydraulic infrastructure began to crumble (canals and dams)... These were the classic manifestations of an exhausted dynasty, making themselves felt since the end of the Qianlong reign (1736–1796/99); they were to impede considerably successors' attempts at reform. Some local functionaries and notables did succeed in tapping

THE GREAT MASSACRE OF THE HUNGRY

The French historian, Emmanuel Leroy-Ladurie, researched the effects of famine, disease, and political, and military chaos in medieval Languedoc, on a fragile population whose growth had tipped the balance toward strained resources. As a result of similar pressure in China, population actually decreased by at least fifty million in the twenty years following 1850 (from 400 to 350 million). Even though growth resumed after 1870, many Chinese feared the imminent extinction of their race, at a time when Westerners were already making inroads in China. Sun Yat-sen and Mao would echo this concern all the way into the 20th century. The 1953 census revealed a reassuring 583 million people, exceeding all estimations. But the memory of the trauma was persistent, and became one of the main issues of Chinese nationalism, contributing considerably, in fact, to its radicalization. It is also behind Mao's tragic mistake to postpone by one generation the implementation of a birth control policy, turning the human weal that was a legacy of the pre-modern epoch into China's biggest obstacle to development. ■

*P*rint from a drawing (China, ca. 1870). Bibliothèque des Arts Décoratifs, Paris.
Ph. © J-L. Charmet.

community networks to make up for the State's shortcomings. But the social fabric had degenerated to a point where the center could no longer hold. The gentry's resources and energies soon had to be directed toward the dangerous threat of rebellion.

Rebellion and Military Buildup

The administrative and social crisis in China created a vacuum that various forms of local solidarity and power tried to fill. Ancient sects and secret societies that exploited the ambient fear and unrest saw their numbers increase dramatically during the 19th century. In the areas where ethnic Chinese were recent arrivals, these conflicts pitted the colonists against the local people. Both communities organized militias for self-defense. This mobilization was often the work of religious sects who acted as intermediaries between notables and defaulting administrators by relying on two important elements of popular culture: the practice of martial arts and religious beliefs. Some sects were able to array vast organizational capacities and ideological indoctrination; chronic unrest was on its way to becoming large-scale rebellion. The White Lotus, active in the Yang-Tse valley from 1796–1805, or the Taiping (1851–1864) are examples.

The chaotic militarization of Chinese society was an inevitable consequence of repeated rebellion, with local militias replacing the military and even the administration: in the Hunan region for example, Zeng Guofan (1811–1872) put together an army to defeat the Taiping, 40 years before the birth of Mao, crushing them in 1864. The communists themselves would encounter a society just as militarized as then, for the institutions and practices remained in place well after the rebellions were quelled, and were appropriated by the warlords when the Empire fell.

The reunification of China under Chiang Kai-shek in 1927–28 had no effect on this state of affairs. The mobilization of strong local structures, of pockets of power in the general chaos, was a technique that Mao used to ensure his rural power base, the long-term pattern that would put power "at the end of the gun." He analyzed the situation in 1928, explaining

*S*muggled opium destabilized international trade, currency (silver gained, while copper lost) and the fiscal system (increase of levies due in silver), the urban economy (in recession from 1820 onwards), and unwound the social fabric.
Ph. © Keystone

communist influence in the countryside as a direct result of the power vacuum. The popular novels he might have read in his youth included *Water Margin* and *The Three Kingdoms*, which portray righteous bandits and rebels, and their foes (corrupt government officials) in a fable of virtuous and fraternal power restored. Of course, he was also influenced by the activist mentality of progressive mandarins, many of whose ideas passed into 20th-century revolutionary thinking.

Begun in the delta region of Canton well before the arrival of Western powers in China, Christianization meant conversions (Emperor Taiping Hong Xiuquan, Dr. Sun Yat-sen), but also virulent rejection in many areas. Anti-missionary violence was one of the main causes of the Second Opium War 1857–60, when this photo was taken) and many other Western incursions in China before the Boxer Rebellion in 1900.

Ph © Roger-Viollet

The Two Sources of Maoism

Rebellion targeted all centers of power—all the cities, institutions, mandarins, and officers thought to be corrupt. A whole set of countervalues was put forth in the sworn brotherhood and solidarity of the warrior, creating a veritable cult of fighting and violence in an attempt to reject the corruption and false honor of the mandarin class. But the rebels were themselves power-hungry. Obsessed with matters of hierarchy, they looked on the masses they mobilized with contempt. Popular novels of the day satirized this penchant for protocol. Nevertheless, the rebellion posed a real threat to the empire, from several perspectives. First, its proclaimed loyalty to the "good" emperor, misled by "bad" ministers, is a classic paradigm. *Water Margin* ends in an amnesty, with the submission of Song Jiang, but there is a darker note in the rejection of Li Kiu, whom the emperor sees brandishing a hatchet against him in a dream. The authorities displayed no less ambiguity in their tacit approval, at times, of the opposition between emperor and ministers. But a purified and reborn empire was forced to demand virtue of its ministers, to prevent the rebellion from taking on an even more dangerous legitimacy.

A common theme was prevalent: the corrupt and destructive nature of power, against which it is necessary to take unrelenting action, either by

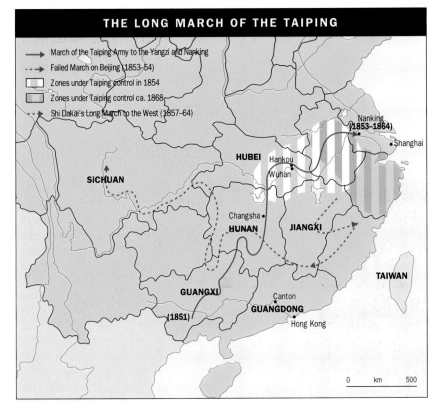

THE LONG MARCH OF THE TAIPING

→ March of the Taiping Army to the Yangzi and Nanking
⇢ Failed March on Beijing (1853–54)
▢ Zones under Taiping control in 1854
▢ Zones under Taiping control ca. 1868
⇢ Shi Dakai's Long March to the West (1857–64)

Nanking (1853–1864)
Shanghai
HUBEI Hankou
Wuhan
SICHUAN
Changsha
HUNAN JIANGXI
TAIWAN
GUANGXI
Canton
GUANGDONG
Hong Kong
(1851)

0 km 500

"virtuous" service to the government or through rebellion. The new mandarins tended not to justify this latter course of action throughout the 19th century, but while supporting the dynasty against the rebels, they carved an alternate path, investing in education, improving the administration and encouraging the citizenry they were in charge of to engage in economic activity. Thus was affirmed, in reaction to an inept bureaucracy and government—not against them but parallel to them—an activist role for the notable class.

Nineteenth-century thinkers insist on the importance of the practical, indeed the physical dimension of political action and the kind of will necessary to undertake it. Individual and collective energies need to be mobilized to ensure the material and moral life (*minsheng*) of the people and to carry out its renovation (*xinmin*), in order to preserve the Empire from death. By example, Zeng Guofang bridged the gap between

The Taiping won many followers among central China's peasants thanks to an egalitarian and anti-Confucian Christianity. But they were doomed by war and internecine quarrels. Shi Dakai's Long March to the West, precursor of Mao's, did not succeed.

the man of action and the scholar. Activism meant that institutional activity had a prestige and a moralizing, mobilizing energy that redeemed its clumsiness. Men of action could be at the same time within a power structure and independent of it, wield authority and criticize it, and in this respect it became an attractive ideal for many 20th-century revolutionaries. So much so that the so–called quest for new institutions based on Western ideologies that they claimed to espouse in their speeches was ultimately much less important than this cult of personal activism. Mao inherited these high expectations of power and used them to justify his own position as a rebel, then his legitimacy as a ruler, to the full extent that his love of authority required. He would not hesitate to act upon society itself, to make it act, and to undermine all opposition.

The weight of this legacy does not make Mao a mere figurehead in the dynastic cycle, for the opening up of the Empire to the West had created an entirely new context.

Adapt to Survive

The First Opium War (1839–42), a result of the Chinese administration's failure to resolve the scandalous trade in the drug, ended in the "unequal treaties." The court ceded Hong Kong to the British, and opened its harbors with special status for foreign boats (limited tariffs and duties). Great Britain, France and Russia each took a piece of the empire. Japan jumped on board in 1895. That year the Treaty of Shimonoseki ratified Japanese control over Taiwan, as well as other territories and privileges. There was another rush for concessions in 1898 that put the Empire on the brink of dismemberment. Fortunately, the imperialists' own rivalries, coupled with tenacious Chinese resistance, enabled the Empire to avoid a total breakup, even after the crushed Boxer Rebellion of 1900. European powers were content to profit by the considerable rights and privileges guaranteed by the treaties, which they enjoyed until 1943. Japan continued its efforts to acquire territory, starting with its defeat of Russian aims in 1905. It obtained further concessions from the Chinese authorities after the

The story of the popular novel *The Water Margin* prefigures Mao's own life, for one of the protagonists escapes, like Mao himself in 1936, toward the Yanan. Works with these rebel heros had existed since the 14th century; they relate episodes of the rebellion at the end of the Song Dynasty (12th century). Shi Jin, honest defender of order, takes up the fight against banditism, before being himself provoked to rebellion by the intrigue of evil functionaries.

"He then told the farm laborers to select two fat buffaloes and kill them; and bring the best brew of the village. He sent invitations to all the Shih clan and upon arrival they seated themselves in order of seniority. Wine was served and Shih Chin then spoke to the audience, saying, 'I have heard there are three robbers on Shao Hwa Shan [...] Sooner or later they will come and pillage our village. I now invite you here to discuss this matter—so that we may be prepared when they come. I will have a rattle sounded at my house when they arrive; and upon hearing this you must bring your arms to defend the village. If your families are attacked we will defend you.' All of them agreed to what Shih Chin said. They then returned home and prepared their weapons. Shih Chin repaired the defenses of the village. [...]

The brigands' approach was duly reported to Shih Chin, who instantly had the rattles sounded and quickly all the men assembled in arms. Shih Chin wore a towel round his head and was equipped with red mail over an embroidered black wadded coat. On his feet were embroidered green boots and round his waist a leather belt. In front and behind were round metal plates. He carried a bow

with quiver full of arrows. In his hand he held a double-edged sword with three-sharp spikes at the end and four holes with eight rings attached. He was mounted on a roan horse. Before him were forty of his retainers while behind him were ninety of the farm laborers. With a combined shout they all moved toward the north end of the village. The brigands halted. Shih Chin saw that Chen Da was in front of his men, wearing a red cap with a concave top, and with iron-mail armor covered with gilt, wadded red clothing, thick army boots and a plaited waistband. He rode a white horse and carried a three-pronged halberd which was about ten feet long. As the two leaders met, then men raised a loud shout. Chen Da paid his respect to Shih Chin by rising in his stirrups." (pages 13–15).

Extract from *Water Margin* by Shih Nai-an. Translated by J.H. Jackson. C & T Co, Cambridge, MA, 1976. Originally published by the Commercial Press, LTD., Shanghai, 1937. ∎

The Second Opium War, waged by the French and British from 1857–60, was to open new ports in the North. Near Beijing, as the fortifications were overrun by the allied troops, the Summer Palace was sacked.
Ph © LL. Viollet

collapse of the Empire, then moved to invade China in 1937. This war played perfectly into Mao's hands, just as the first Sino-Japanese War contributed to an upsurge of nationalism, reform, and revolution, by preventing the restoration from taking hold after the initial defeat of the rebels.

Contrary to Japan, which implemented radical reforms during the Meiji period after 1868, China postponed transforming institutions until 1901, when it was forced to by foreign powers. During the period 1860–95, the men of the restoration— functionaries in Beijing and the provinces—went about improving certain key areas such as defense, diplomacy, transportation, and industry. The West's military and commercial superiority had made its impression, and the Chinese sought to appropriate whatever they could in a practical way. But they were determined to keep society, art and the institutions in line with the basic principles of Chinese civilization. Western civilization, in spite of its industrial strength, was not considered superior; on the contrary, westerners were barbarians. With this unshakeable confidence, China rapidly rebounded, and the renovation of the moral climate allowed China to regain the upper hand.

It is worth noting two constants that would carry over into Mao's time: selective westernization in the service of national aims and values, and the Great Leap Forward syndrome as the initial reaction to Western incursions. There would be a series of Great Leaps as the seriousness of the crisis increased; Mao was born into a time of accelerating history.

The Treaty of Shimonoseki was the death knell of conservative restoration with its selective borrowing of Western practices. The traditionalists criticized the cost and inefficiency of reforms that didn't protect China from defeat. The reformers wanted to redefine the very essence of Chinese society, like the Japanese had done, on a double base of industrial progress and nationalism. These two sides polarized China in the 1890s in a bitter debate.

A good portion of notables, members of sects and secret societies, and the administration came out in favor of traditional values, and of the ultraconservative faction that had taken power with the approval of Cixi. Fear and rejection of foreigners brought many sects closer to their usual enemy, officialdom. The Boxers and the Court formed an alliance in 1900 against the Western powers. But defeat forced Cixi to accept the modernization program of the reformers, with whom a great many Chinese identified.

Contrary to the traditionalists, the reformers had limited assets in the years 1870–80. In the spheres of power, there were a few enlightened functionaries, who had been on diplomatic missions to the West and seen the benefits of representative government. There were also the port zones, where a new urban elite was learning professional politics—among whom one Sun Yat-sen, a doctor of medicine from Hong Kong. From 1890 onwards, the influence of the coastal areas along with the areas' reformist ideas began to reach the towns of the interior. An example is Changsha, the

In some of the open ports, Westerners used their privilege of extraterritoriality, which meant that Chinese law did not apply to them, to equip and administer their concessions as in the West. Reformers pointed to these areas (below, in Beijing) as examples of development.
Ph © Boyer-Viollet

capital of Hunan province, not too far from Mao's birthplace. Activism politicized notables everywhere. Neither the failure of the Hundred Days reforms of 1898 (see p. 34), nor the traditionalist offensive two years later slowed the impetus of the reformers. From 1901 onward, the notables participated in the elaboration of reforms accepted by Cixi. The education system was restructured, exams and statutes of the mandarin society were abolished (1905), and all of this worked toward creating a more open, diverse, and professionalized society. By giving university students, as well as military officers, a Western-style education, the reformers provided them with the skills necessary to take up the Nationalist cause and be of service to the state. Indeed, the first generation of intellec-tuals and soldiers who were trained at the reformed schools at the beginning of the 20th century were the leaders of the communist revolution. In the meantime, failure was to befall the generation immediately preceding them, the generation responsible for the end of the Empire.

Attacks against foreigners and against modernity: here a Boxer image shows the sacrifice of the Christian pig and the foreign goat. Other targets included telegraphic installations (the first line was laid between Shanghai and Tianjin in 1879), railroads (the first foreign segment, illegally built at the doors of Shanghai, was interrupted in 1978), factories, machines, and even, after 1900, police headquarters.
Ph © J.-L. Charmet

The Short Spring of the Republic (1912)

In the early 1900s, the unique political landscape that emerged was centered around the interplay between the notables' administrative or professional associations, groups of students, military officers and revolutionaries. This dynamic was held together by nationalism, aimed not only at foreigners but also at the Manchu Qing dynasty, the principal enemy of Dr. Sun Yat-sen and the republicans. The most decisive opposition, however, came from the more moderate quarters among the notables. The revolutionaries fanned the flames, but their own divisions—as well as vigorous repression—would prevent them from playing a major part in the uprising. The immediate cause was the split between the successors of Cixi (who had died in 1908) and the notables. The former attempted to restore central authority by streamlining the administration and rationalizing (by way of nationalization) the railroads, which had sprouted in every province as works of patriotic fervor. The ambition of the notables was to go beyond the provinces, to participate in the national power structure in Beijing.

The tendency to reform mobilized the notables against the weakened central authority, which appeared to be implementing reforms only to keep a hold on power. By 1908, the conflict polarized malcontents of all types. In the central and southern provinces, the unrest assembled partisans of the constitutional monarchy (often urban notables), together with republican revolutionaries (often students or officers affiliated with Dr. Sun Yat-sen's Sworn League—see p. 37), and anyone else who didn't like the Manchus—conservative notables, sects, and secret societies. A formidable, but fragile and diverse coalition, which could possibly defeat the power in place, but hardly create a new political system.

The regents governing for the young Emperor Pu Yi since 1908 got things started by allowing elections for

Originally from Shandong province, the Boxers invaded Beijing and besieged the diplomatic quarter, with the approval of the Court. They were crushed by a foreign expeditionary force, which imposed a new "Unequal Treaty" and stiff reparations. The repression was extremely violent, as were the attacks by Boxers against missionaries and especially against Chinese converts.
Ph © Edimédia

THE REFORMISTS AND THE HUNDRED DAYS

Toward the end of the 19th century, reformist thinkers leaned toward economic modernization and repre-sentative government. Kang Youwei's (1858–1927) plan included a mandarin assembly, reforming the exam system, as well as an ambitious public works program (transportation, port improvement, etc.). Liang Qichao (1873–1927) laid the foundations of modern nationalism, by convincing the elite to be loyal to the nation, rather than to the dynasty, and pinpointing the precise threat the West posed to China. It was not only, as many thought, that its essence, institutions and culture were endangered, but even its independence and national sovereignty. Liang was influenced by Darwinism, and recognized that progress meant abandoning certain traditions: the educational system had to be modernized, women emancipated, the practice of foot-binding abolished. Emphasis on reform as a means to save the country would become the norm later with the "cultural revolutions" that punctuated 20th-century China. But most 1890 reformers' ideas were a far cry from the iconoclastic fervor of the future revolutionaries; only Tan Sitong (1865–1898) championed "total" westernization. The reformists' style reflected the gradual evolution of the notables' status, and they imitated the latters' associative, activist methods. Their liberal discourse was often a front for pre-existing agendas of local autonomy, and democracy was conceived as a kind of paternalistic education of the people under the wing of the elite. The reinforcing of power was one of the modernizers' top priorities: Kang and Liang popularized the idea of an enlightened despot that attracted many, including the young Mao—who hastened to enrich his pantheon of ancient Chinese heroes with figures like Peter the Great and Napoleon. It is clear that the politicization of mandarin activists did not lead to the creation of an independent political arena. Kang, Liang, and Tan all had Beijing-based careers, and were under the protective umbrella of the bureaucracy or the imperial administration. The young Emperor Guangxu (whose regent was Cixi) called on them to head a reform drive, during the panic of the race for concessions in June 1898. One hundred days of reforms ensued before Cixi's counterattack. The regent and her "ultras" succeeded in forcing Kang and Liang into exile in Japan; Tan Sitong let himself be captured and executed along with other revolutionary leaders. This heroic self-sacrifice became an inspiration for the next gener-ation of anti-Manchu rebels. ∎

Ph © Harlingue-Viollet

provincial assemblies, while postponing the constitutional reforms promised by Cixi (1909). These assemblies became hotbeds of opposition. During the summer of 1911, Sichuan province joined the dissidents. On October 10th ("Double Ten Day"), a group of low-ranking officers staged a coup in Wuchang, capital of the neighboring province of Hubei. Without being part of the Sworn League, they were influenced by its propaganda. The insurgents proclaimed the provincial assembly of notables as sole authority. Independent republics were declared in quick succession in the central and southern provinces, following Hubei's example. The notables took charge of these decentralized revolutions, and the Sworn League was conspicuous in its absence, although Sun Yat-sen hastened to return from the United States. The League would make its voice heard in Canton and Shanghai, and within the assembly of provincial delegates that gathered at Nanking, obtaining the election of Sun Yat-sen to the Presidency of the Republic on January 1, 1912.

In the meantime, Beijing responded by launching a military offensive against the South, led by Yuan Shikai's Beiyang army. The balance of power between North and South soon imposed a compromise: Yuan Shikai negotiated the abdication of Pu Yi, the "last emperor"; in exchange, Sun Yat-sen stepped down in favor of Yuan. In March, he became president of a seemingly republican and reunified China—but, in fact, of a China threatened by fragmentation and reactionary forces. The revolutionaries were disorganized, but this was only one of many signs of weakness among the political forces in play. Neither the parliament nor the parties (such as the Nationalist Guomindang Party, successor of the League) were reinforced by the elections of 1912. Power ended up in the hands of the only faction that could ensure national cohesion: the Beiyang army, supported politically and financially by the foreign Alliance. After the Guomindang victory, Yuan crushed southern revolts against his authoritarian plans, proclaimed himself dictator in 1914, and tried to restore the Empire in 1915, provoking in his turn a rebellion that quickly bogged down in the provinces,

Before taking over the Presidency of the Republic in 1912 from Sun Yat-sen, General Yuan Shikai (1859–1916) was the main architect of military reform. The Northern Army, called the Beiyang Army, was intensely loyal to him. After Yuan's death, the warlords from its ranks would divide up China among themselves.
Ph © Coll. Viollet

like the one two years previously. Following Yuan's demise in 1916, the military fell apart, to the benefit of a myriad group of warlords. The parliamentary framework and the central government, both ineffectual but surviving in Beijing, could not hide the increasing fragmentation of a country that was retreating within local boundaries. The dream was short-lived, but in 1912, the Republic still projected an aura of solidity, freedom and opportunities for military-minded people. A naïve and fervent eighteen-year-old, Mao Zedong, answered the call.

*F*rom the Taiping to the Boxers, violence becomes part of political life in the Empire. Pursued, murdered, the anti-Manchu revolutionaries espoused violence with quasi-religious zeal. The communists and Mao found this warrior spirit intact in the 1920s.
Ph © Roger-Viollet

SUN YAT-SEN AND THE ANTI-MANCHU REVOLUTIONARIES

A native of the delta region of Canton, Dr. Sun Yat-sen was an early proponent of violent opposition to the throne. In 1895, following Shimonoseki, his group of revolutionaries were average rebels, recruited similarly to those of the southern secret societies. But Sun was to quickly extend his power base to Christian Chinese and Chinese of the diaspora (in the West Indies and Indochina). Absorbed by incessant intrigues and plotting in southern China, Sun had some trouble making his voice heard among republican groups that sprouted up after 1900. His role seems to have been more to represent the ideal, professional revolutionary. He finally managed to federate his movement in 1905 as the "Sworn League" with its vague program of "Three Principles of the People." Anti-Manchu nationalism went hand in hand with cooperation with the West and even attempts at rapprochement with Japan. The Republic itself was modeled after the American political system. A social agenda called the "Life of the People" mixed traditional ideals such as land redistribution with a special brand of industrialization, that was supposed to avoid the usual pitfalls of capitalism thanks to state intervention. Like all his contemporaries, Sun wanted economic progress without the class struggle. But his vision of the State as watchdog marginalized him as the more

activist convictions of intellectuals took to the fore. For them, democracy was the pure expression of the people's free will, united around the avant-garde, opposite the political institutions, represented by the hated Qing regime, and representing, to the people's eyes, alienating cleavages and corruption. The prevailing model in the minds of the first

revolutionaries, a fusion of the rebel and activist ideals, was a social and democratic state, self-managed by the people under the "heroic" leadership of the intellectuals. This special vision of democracy had a long life span, well beyond as a reactive interpretation of Western ideologies. Unsurprisingly, many of its proponents were nihilists, anarchists, or

populists. In other words, they were partisans of a variety of community-based organizational structures, and often saw violence as a form of heroic individualism—like the much-admired original Russian revolutionaries. This is certainly what doomed the 1905 union, and even the party. Sun failed to impose his institutional policies on the activist chaos, which nevertheless was more connected to society. As the modernization of China progressed, Sun was left behind. His reign lasted no more than three months in 1912. ■

Ph © L'Illustration/Sygma

Chapter 2

A COUNTRY BOY
BETWEEN TWO CHINAS

1893–1920

THE SON OF A PEASANT, MAO ZEDONG COMPLETED HIS FIRST APPRENTICESHIP IN POLITICS AT CHANGSHA, CAPITAL OF HUNAN PROVINCE. FROM THE BIRTH OF A REPUBLIC TO THE FOUNDATION OF THE COMMUNIST PARTY, MAO CLIMBED THE RANKS AS A RURAL AGITATOR.

I n the aftermath of the Double Ten, Mao sought to join Hubei's troops. Rebellion had already erupted at Changsha on October 22. Mao joined the army of Tan Yankai, a future provincial warlord, staying with the Hunanese for the few months necessary for Tan to liquidate the agitators of the Sworn League— the very ones who had helped him take power. The fact that the social, political, and military elite were in control of the Republic didn't bother the young Mao: in the spring of 1922, the revolution was over for him, and he left the army. The older Mao would not have been so naïve, but his younger self was a mirror of the epoch, of its hopes and its illusions.

The 1936 autobiography dictated to Edgar Snow, an American journalist, is a politicized version of Mao Zedong's childhood and adolescence. His parents were complete opposites: a greedy father who became rich in the grain trade and a tender, pious Buddhist mother, with whom the young Mao sided against his father's authority. At age eight (1902), as was the custom, he began the study of Chinese writing and the classics of Chinese literature. Going to school didn't save him from work in the fields, however; his family had neither the traditional ways nor the means of the lettered class. Mao's father wanted a successor—that is, an accountant. And what were the classics worth anyway, since exams had been done away with? In 1907, Mao was taken out of school and set to work in the fields and on the books. The career of a small-time manager,

Mao Zedong (third from the left) was born on December 26th 1893 in the village of Shaoshan, in the Xiantang district of Hunan Province, a rural area at the geographic center of the Qing Empire. He was a son of the earth, like the 400 million others who constitued the majority of Cixi's and her nephew Guangxu's (the next to last Son of the Heavens) subjects.
Ph © R. Burri/Magnum

Mao (right) grew up in a peasant household, with a father who had become rich as a grain merchant, and who wanted his son to be a bookkeeper. Mao vehemently rejected his authority.
Ph © R. Burri/Magnum

an atom in the growing galaxy of rural petite bourgeoisie, held little attraction to the boy who would condemn this class in pure Marxist form twenty years later. He took his education upon himself, was tutored by a student and an old mandarin, and secretly read popular novels that put him in touch with the hero ethic and inspired him with the sound of the times: a call for the regeneration of China.

Apprenticeship

Acquiring new knowledge became Mao's priority. His desire to enroll in one of the schools opened by Hunan notables, active in educational reform, infuriated his father. Mao refused to yield, and 1910 found him a student in the district capital of Xiangxiang, adjacent to the Xiangtan district, where his mother came from. At sixteen, he not only discovered independence, but also a wider perspective on the national crisis. After learning of the death of Cixi two years late, he caught up with the reform movement. The exploits of Kang Youwei and Liang Qichao thrilled him, and while he shuddered at the fate of Korea (colonized by the Japanese in 1910), he applauded the victory of the Japanese over the Russians in 1905. Besides novels, Mao read biographies of great men, such as Rousseau, Lincoln, Napoleon, and Zeng Guofan—in other words philosophers, statesmen, founders, or "restorers" of empires. In 1911, he went to the capital of Hunan Province, Changsha, to attend high school.

Mao the vague reformist and budding Nationalist was soon to assert his rebel streak under the influence of his republican comrades. With them he wrote out proclamations, which they proudly plastered on the walls of the school (the famous *dazibaos* of the Cultural Revolution originated in these anonymous traditions). Like them he cut off his braid, the symbol of his status as a Qing subject. Rather than think about the revolution, he acted—convincing others, even the most hesitant of his classmates, to do so as well. This in itself does not presage Mao's leadership qualities, for such anti-Manchu bravado was in the air in 1911.

But Mao studied the popular hero ethic closely, and was already imagining himself as both a rebel and a statesman—or at any rate, as a warlord, not a mandarin. Conforming to the ideals of his time, he placed the force of will and physical and moral courage above thought and ideas. Communism would leave this important character trait intact, while giving him the added weapon of ideological dogmatism. Like many revolutionaries, Mao Zedong had an instinctive mistrust of institutional structures, and so oscillated between destructive rebellion and perfectionist activism.

In 1912, the success of the Revolution briefly suspended Mao's wariness. The Republic seemed to propose a framework that was favorable to the emancipation of society. Entering politics at this time, Mao was armed with little besides his personal synthesis of the rebel-hero ideal and a sense of imperial grandeur. The human factor, in his view, would triumph over political contradictions. Aware of the rift between revolutionaries and reformers, but unable to

View of a village taken from the Beijing-Hanku railway, end of the 19th century. In spite of a lively coastal trade, the Empire's economy was mostly agrarian. Mao didn't need to "discover" rural reality; unlike European intellectuals, Chinese revolutionaries had never forgotten their peasant roots. Ph © M. Durazzo/ANA

choose between two equally compelling paths, he envisioned a China ruled by a triumvirate: Sun Yat-sen, Kang Youwei, and Liang Qichao.

Toward Another Revolution

The failure of the Republic shattered these illusions. Intellectuals abandoned institutional politics to devote themselves to grassroots activities (cooperatives, education) or new forms of expression such as demonstrations and strikes. The social radicalism of the anti-Qing movement of the 1900 years was even stronger after 1910. Mao turned to this new kind of activism, which rejected politics, with its violence and plots, to better unite with the "masses"—the Marxist term fit the Chinese people well.

This renewal was enabled by two concurrent phenomena: the extraordinary development of urban society in the coastal regions, and the coming of age of a new generation of intellectuals. Toward 1915, industrialization started to take off in China thanks to a favorable economy and the collapse of the central government, which reduced bureaucratic obstacles. Caught up in World War I, Europeans had left open certain sectors such as textiles—and the US and Japan could not by themselves satisfy world demand. Production and exports boomed, a situation that would last until the early 1920s.

With its entrepreneurial bourgeoisie, its industrial areas where factories and workers' quarters grew side by side, its quickly modernizing social movements—spawning unions, citizens' associations, strikes, and demonstrations—"Blue" China was seeking and finding modernity. Intellectuals had a new audience that reached far beyond the politicized, graduating classes of the first modernized schools. Indeed, a new enemy appeared

THE UNIVERSE OF MAO

Yangtze River

HUBEI

SICHUAN

Dongting Lake

Changsha ▣

H U N A N

Xiangtan •

Xiang-Xiang •

JIANGXI

GUIZHOU

Xiang River

GUANGXI

GUANGDONG

0   km   200

Contrary to the peasant universe of Shaoshan and Xiangtan, Changsha was a big city, although a provincial one compared to Beijing or Shanghai. But Changsha was open to diverse political currents; the memory of Zeng Guofan (a statesman who had crushed the Taiping in 1864) was strong, as was that of the reformers, Liang Qichao and Tan Sitong, who had fought their first battles in the Hunan before the Hundred Days of 1898.

on the scene, crystallizing intellectual animosity, diverting it from the anti-Qing violence of the previous generation to take on the whole series of traditions and customs that was Confucianism.

At the fore of anti-Confucian sentiment, there was a man, Chen Duxiu (1879–1942); a review, *New*

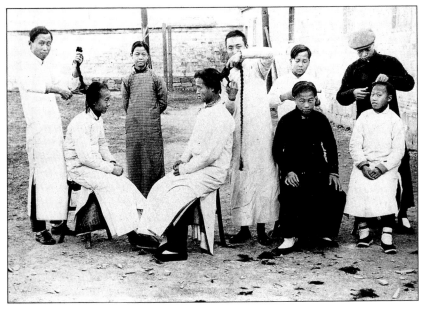

Youth, that Chen, an ardent Francophile, had founded in Shanghai in 1915; and an idea: the failure of the Republic was due to moral and mental causes. Contrary to Sun Yat-sen, whose recipe for progress was political and military, Chen Duxiu designated a much more potent enemy than the Qing dynasty—Confucius—as the root of the evils of bureaucracy, militarism, and the injustices of a conformist, passive society. Chinese youth, not yet broken by these evils and capable of enthusiasm, was called upon by Chen to destroy the idols of a defunct order and free itself in the name of democracy and science.

Chen and his friends (notably Hu Shi) propounded an activist renewal in order to establish a society able to support the institutions of a liberal democracy that

The braid was imposed on Chinese men by Manchu conquerors in the 17th century. Cutting it signified sympathy for the revolutionary cause in the 1900s and, more generally, for the movement of China's renewal.
Ph © Edimédia

From around 1915, "Blue" China experienced a Golden Age, which, while it lacked the support of solid political institutions, had a decisive effect on the modernization of the big coastal cities, especially Shanghai—here, seen from the Bund, the main road through the commercial district that follows a curve of the Hwang-Po River, at the junction of the French and International Concessions.
Ph © Roger-Viollet

would guarantee the rights of the individual. While politically aware young people were receptive to this message of personal liberation, there was also a deep mistrust of politics due to war (in China and in Europe), imperialism, political maneuvering and corruption, which discouraged them from thinking about the instruments of democracy (such as political parties or human rights, in the juridical sense of the term). In keeping with the anti-Qing revolutionary ethos, "democracy" referred to the unity of the nation and its people, led by its avant-garde (students and intellectuals) against a bad government.

Being a democrat meant being a social patriot; freeing oneself meant living freely, often by refusing marriage or a career mapped out by one's parents. In groups or in reviews, people debated how to "save China" and organized collective action among students and the masses. These demonstrations were often of a local nature, centered around local interests such as defending the provinces against military cliques or protecting businesses coveted by capitalists based outside these provinces. The radicals courted

moderate notables and reformers—those who were the driving force behind the provincial movements that sought autonomy. They also established alliances with local warlords, considered legitimate allies because they came from the region and were "patriots." Beyond this local horizon—within which Mao was still ensconced—another kind of radicalism was burgeoning in the big cities and within national movements. Its target was foreign aggression, in particular Japan's. In May 1919, the Treaty of Versailles ceded to the Japanese German concessions in Shandong Province. In response, students in Beijing demonstrated, spurring a wave of patriotic protest joined by merchants and factory workers and resulting in the famous May 4th Movement.

This movement gave a powerful boost to community-oriented activism. The rich were called upon to help the poor. People banded together in cooperative structures; students went to the villages to instruct the "masses," while educating themselves through contact with the workers in the factories and the fields. The new ideal was a union of work and knowledge. Manual labor was declared "sacred," but science and technology were worshipped at the same altar. These themes held a renewed, lasting influence over anarchists, who lured to France several thousand "student-workers" and inspired attempts at communal existence in China.

This climate of optimism and concord soon darkened. Unrelenting war in a disintegrated and impotent China, and the increasing gravity of worker unrest, caused people to doubt the capacity of the new activism to achieve reformist goals. The Russian Revolution's delayed impact further intensified uncertainty. Could poverty be overcome, and could the Chinese people (women included) be liberated through grassroots action and education? Could China survive with cooperatives as the only form of government? Could power be won simply by taking to the streets? Which of the newly discovered thinkers of Western Enlightenment—which Rousseau, Tolstoy, Marx, Proudhon, Sorel, Dewey, or Russell—would be the guiding light for the new China?

"**D**own with Confucius' boutique!" In New Youth, then from his professorship at Beijing University, Chen Duxiu called on young Chinese to become acquainted with modernity through two "gentlemen": "Mr. Science" and "Mr. Democracy." He encouraged them to develop self-reliance in their lives (by choosing their spouse or their career) and rejected the moral dimension dear to Confucius, in which he saw only servitude. Ph © Edimédia

*"**S**ave our homeland!" Like the generation of revolutionaries at the end of the Empire, those of "May 4th" were united by a fervent naitonalism. Here, in discussion with the Beijing police, a group of students call for a boycott on Japanese products.*

Ph © Edimédia

The generation of the May 4th Movement subjected an entire culture of left-wing thought to intense scrutiny, and found there—not without trepidation—the looming necessity of revolution, of a radical and concerted rupture with the accepted order of things. Some resisted drawing this conclusion; the broadly influential and highly diverse reformist tendency refused to divide China into social classes, political parties, or ideological factions. The radicals, to the contrary, insisted on the global and revolutionary character of the renewed society they envisioned. Most divisive was the question of method—whether to organize structured political parties, whether to use violent means, whether to link political protestation and social unrest together in the revolutionary process.

Only a handful leaned toward the Bolshevik model. But this handful—around 60 individuals—former anti-Confucianists converted in 1919–20, were to lay the foundations of Chinese communism. Lenin's ideas were adapted and betrayed by Mao's generation, just as Mao's would be in the West by the generation of the sixties (see p. 49).

The first communists intended on emulating as scrupulously as possible the basis of the Bolshevik model; i.e., the transformation of the working class into an operational political force. They formed small groups within the associations that arose after May 4th in most of China's big cities, and among Chinese students in Tokyo and the "worker-students" in Paris. During this period, these groups were precipitated, so to speak, out of splits and purges in the anarchist and Guomindang formations. Sun Yat-sen revived his party in 1920, taking advantage of the organizational fervor to promote ideas diametrically opposed to the communists. He sought to appeal to workers while rejecting the concept of class struggle.

Communist groups in Shanghai (under the leadership of Chen Duxiu) and in Beijing (under Li Dazhao) accepted the help of delegates from the Komintern, the international communist organization founded by Lenin in 1919, to organize worker action and propaganda. In July 1921, Hendricus Sneevliet, also known as Maring, achieved the fusion of these groups. Thirteen delegates, including Mao Zedong from Hunan, from the two groups met in the French

THE MOVEMENT OF MAY 4TH 1919

The Conference of Versailles seemed to have forgotten China's entry into the Great War on the side of the Allies, and remembered previous promises to the Japanese, by granting Japan the Shandong concession. This act, a profound deception for the Chinese Occidentalists, spurred students in Beijing to take to the streets, clamoring their opposition to the Allies, to Japan and to China's militarist government—whose delegates had left Versailles without signing the treaty. Soon, students from other cities joined the movement, and merchant associations and workers organized boycotts and strikes. The movement was repressed, and Chen Duxiu thrown in prison, but in spite of this, what the demonstrators obtained was not negligible: several pro-Japanese ministers in the government resigned, and vernacular Chinese was introduced into the educational system. More significantly, the revolutionary fever that drove the movement, the agitation of ideas and the political articulation resulted in the creation of the Communist Party in 1921, and the rebirth of Sun Yat-sen's Guomindang. Dr. Sun seized the opportunity to return to the forefront of the political arena, while avoiding Chen's rejection of traditions. These parties would connect with reformers in the provinces, re-establishing a form of national politics. "Blue" China, and its intellectual and social ferment, thus expanded its influence into the mid-1920s, even while economic growth slowed down. ■

concession in Shanghai from July 27–30 to found the Chinese Communist Party. In spite of the police interrupting their work, they proclaimed their adhesion to the Komintern, rejected an alliance with the Guomindang and installed Chen Duxiu as the leader of the new party.

The Student

An elder among the May 4th generation (already twenty when the Qing dynasty and the Republic fell), Mao was on the same wavelength as his contemporaries in his marked preference for the Hunanese city, Changsha. He stopped short of the cosmopolitanism of Beijing and the intellectual atmosphere of Shanghai; viscerally attached to his native Hunan, he gave a distinctly provincial color to the new ideas of the time, and his interpretation of communism. In 1912, after leaving the army, he busied himself perusing the Changsha newspaper ads for vocational schools. Policeman, soap manufacturer, jurist ("mandarin and jurist," is what he wrote to his parents), businessman—which career to choose? Business school bored him after a month. The next six months he spent reading at the Changsha Public Library (where he saw a map of the world for the first time). He finally reassured his parents, who were threatening to cut off his allowance, by enrolling in a Changsha Teacher Training College.

Though hardly a rival to the intellectual cosmopolitanism of Beida (Beijing University), this school dispensed high-level instruction, and Mao felt its echo in *New Youth*, which he started reading in 1916, and in one of his professors, Yang Changji (whose daughter, Yang Kaihui, he would marry in the winter of 1920, bucking his family's plans for an arranged marriage with a peasant girl). An enthusiast of a moderate version of Occidentalism, Yang taught the principles of voluntarism, and encouraged his disciples to find practical solutions to theoretical problems. Mao found in this discourse a confirmation of his own tendencies, and a new legitimacy for his contempt of "pure intellectuals." They, in return, regarded with disdain their aloof

Editor of New Youth, Li Dazhao (1888–1927) was one of the first to become seriously interested in Marxism; his reading of Marx remained however faithful to Chinese revolutionary thought. In his view China's people as a whole, including the peasants, could be seen as the proletariat. In this respect he was no precursor of Mao, but rather a representative of a general tendency shared by all the "converted" Marxists. From France, Cai Hesen wrote to his friend Chen Duxiu in February 1921: "China is an entirely proletarian nation." Ph © Edimédia classmate, older, poorly and simply dressed, a rustic with a big mouth; an eccentric who, to express his physical pride, would walk about naked to show off his muscles. Thanks to Yang, Mao wrote an article published in *New Youth* in April of 1917, "A Study of

LENIN SEEN FROM CHINA

Use the enemy's strength against itself, organize the struggle at all levels of society—these mantras appealed to the anarchists as a validation of the communitarian model. In 1919, Soviet Russia was in the throes of Civil War and famine; Bolshevik organization crystallized into the new, centralized regime that implemented War Communism and quickly supplanted Soviet "democracy." The peaceful solutions of community solidarity and local action central to the Chinese model turned out to be anachronisms in the modern world of organized violence. The theory of the class struggle designated a clearly Chinese enemy: the State, and behind it, the army, which had given the country over to foreign imperialists and international capitalists. The converted Marxists remained strongly attached to the ideal of national unity. They retained from Lenin's thought the fusion of social revolution and national liberation from the imperialist yoke. China was not considered a society of classes (the first class-based analyses would come out in 1923), but a "proletarian nation"; all Chinese were therefore potential revolu-

tionaries. (Li Dazhao was the precursor of this essential idea shared by all the new Marxists, rather than the pre-Maoist some hastily made him out to be.) No less powerful was the identification with the "working class." This was a way of adapting the model of the avant-garde party of the proletariat to the activist ethos that placed the heroes at the reins of power squarely within the people. However, this would be used to justify the separate existence of the party organization and its strategic superiority. Far from being a hastily fashioned hodge-podge, this vision owes its coherence to the "voluntarism" of its proponents. While adopting Lenin's principal axiom (revolution is a product of the dialectical nature of history's unfolding, but it has to be forced into being nevertheless), they infused it with the late 19th-century idealization of will as a driving force, proclaiming the superiority of "subjective" factors. In this respect, political organization of the masses was not only the best way to win power, but also the means to overcome capitalist domination—the old objective of the anti-Manchu revolutionaries, and the hope of the first reformers—through

decisive action. In 1920, Chen Duxiu realized the new movement's potential, and how it resonated with his own faith in the transforming capacity of urbanization and industrialization. The factory, the machine, and their human avatar—the working class—took over the hopes he had first placed in the will of Chinese youth. The old dichotomy of city and country had lost its relevance. Few were those who remained faithful to rural activism: Li Dazhao was alone in attempting to bypass politicizing the working class and apply the new model at the village level. To be sure, there was no orthodoxy among the newly converted Marxists in 1920. How could there have been? In Europe, communism had evolved from a whole culture of workers' movements and left-wing politics. In China, it had to create its own foundation. The 1920s were a decade of ideological progress, but there was still a significant gap between Chinese reality and the Russian model. It would be filled by Maoism. ■

Xiao:—Do you plan to spend your vacation here, at school, like last summer?

Mao:—I haven't decided yet. And you?

Xiao:—Me, I'm going to travel by begging.

Mao:—Begging? What do you mean? I don't understand…"

Xiao Zicheng, 1916.

_____

Physical Education," which was about his athletic version activism.

With two of his classmates, Cai Hesen and Xiao Zicheng, Mao formed the "Heroic Trio," in reference to the popular *Romance of the Three Kingdoms*. Mao put his friends through strenuous toughening exercises. During the summers, the trio hiked the countryside, sleeping under the stars, listening to beggars and storytellers, running away from ferocious dogs the villagers would sometimes set on them. They lived out their desire to keep in touch with the old, traditional China, but they had also defected to the city, embraced modernity and rejected Confucius.

Straddling these two worlds, Mao the student activist started militating for the new ideas, and participated in the creation of an association. In 1917, the year of the "salvos of the October Revolution" he armed his friends with bamboo swords to fight off a raid by local militarist agitators. While others were debating how to save China, Mao rejected politics and the necessary reliance on connections and money, and the ideal of educating the people—far too slow in his view to have an effect. He wanted to imitate the heroes of *Water Margin*.

The next two years set him more firmly on the path to modernity and the city. In a last homage to the old and newer activisms, Mao founded the Association for the Regeneration of the People (Xinmin Xuehui) at his graduation in the spring of 1918, with Cai and a few other "heroic" classmates (among them Liu Shaoqi). Then his old mentor Yang was promoted to

the Beida, and Mao followed him to Beijing. Mao obtained, thanks to Yang, a post at the university library, of which Li Dazhao was in charge. Displaying more benevolence to the young man most others at the Beida dismissed as an incomprehensible rustic, Li invited Mao to what he called the "Red Pavilion," a seminar on Marxism he conducted in the winter of 1918, where he professed an anarchist's vision of the Russian model and encouraged young people to "go out to the villages." Mao did nothing of the sort; he went to Shanghai.

In early 1919, Mao met Hunanese students recruited by the Xinmin Association to join the "student-workers" in France. Other members of the Association, such as Liu Shaoqi, went to Moscow, encouraged by He Minfan, a wily mandarin and one of the first Changsha converts to communism. Mao, however, stayed in the port city, happy to discover urban modernity on Chinese soil—which he wouldn't leave until 1950, the year he met Stalin in Moscow. He was in his native Hunan when the May 4th Movement swept through Changsha. During the summer, he participated in the organization of students, professors, and enlightened local notables. The weekly newspaper he founded, the *Critic of Hunan*, was soon shut down by the local militarists targeted in its fiery editorials. In November 1919, he had to flee. During his second stay in Beijing, he read for the first time translations of Marxist works— in fragments! Then, in Shanghai, while working for a dry cleaner, he met a prestigious figure, Chen Duxiu,

The somber founders of the Chinese Communist Party. Having attended the first party congress was not evidence of any particular historical importance. If it had been executed in 1927 after his arrest by the Hunan rural police, Mao would have been noticed more than the somber delegates from Shandong, Wang Jinmei and Deng Enming. He is flanked by another man from Hunan, He Shuheng, a member of the old generation like Dong Biwu, delegate from Hubei with Chen Tanqiu. Except Maring, head of the first congress, the real founders of the CCP—Li Dazhao and more importantly Chen Duxiu—were absent. From left to right: Mao, Wang Jinmei (1898–1925), Deng Enming (1900–1930), He Shuheng (1874–1935), Dong Biwu (1886–1975), Chen Tanqiu (1896–1943).
Ph © Archives CDCC

who was about to announce his conversion to communism. He was convinced that achieving democracy required a massive, and militarized, party organization. Mao too would come to nearly the same conclusion upon his return to Changsha.

"Marx's Party"

Where was Mao headed? Actually, not to communism, and even less to Marxism per se; rather, a mass activism whose energy was channeled by a solidly-organized party structure—precisely what the small proto-communist groups were against. It was the model that counted, as the letters that Cai Hesen sent Mao from France reveal (see sidebar). The ideologue that Snow comes across in 1936 dates from 1920, and his conversion to a practical and theoretical version of Marxism comes after a short-lived flirtation with the anarchist ideal. Of course, Mao was no more an

THE GREAT UNION OF POPULAR MASSES

During the feverish days of the May 4th Movement, Mao wrote his first theoretical analysis of the revolution, "The Great Union of Popular Masses," and published it in his *Critic of Hunan*. The high stakes and important choices were clearly outlined: Mao presented Marxism as a violent strategy that entailed using the methods of the enemy to destroy "capitalists and aristocrats." Inspired by Kropotkin and Proudhon, favorites of the Chinese anarchists, he encouraged solidarity and a reformist outlook. He praised in loving terms the guilds, merchant associations, student groups, and trade unions as evidence of the Chinese talent for unity against militarism and imperialism.

The peasants were included in this "great union," but the dynamism and the initiative should come from the big cities. This is a remarkable document, one of the few that show a Mao not taken with power and combat, but a Mao who disdained violence. Other activists of the May 4th Movement saw that the crucial actors in society were no longer the mythified People, Race, or Heroes. The student, the merchant, the worker, the woman, and the peasant possessed the power that could be harnessed to "save" China—and the provinces.

For Mao, the province of Hunan was the top priority. The passage to communism meant taking voluntarism one step further, to political institutions. Chen Duxiu probably laid out this theory to

Mao in the winter of 1920. Then, from France, Cai Huisen, converted in the spring of 1920, also declared: Forget the Hunan! Forget solidarity! What is necessary is to organize a party at the national level, create a powerful tool of clandestine struggle, and choose sides. In July 1920, Xiao Zicheng wrote to Mao: "I chose Proudhon; Cai chose Marx." Between Cai's vision and what Mao was to do in the Hunan, there was a vast gap—but a decisive step had been taken. ∎

anarchist in 1919 than a communist in 1920. What he was reneging was his belief in "autonomous" social activism, a faith shared by all his contemporaries; the one he expressed in the "Great Union of Popular Masses" in 1919. From 1920 on, his plan was to incarnate the Great Union in a party.

This marked the true entry of Mao into politics, for which the spontaneous organization of 1911–12, forgotten in the enthusiasm of the intervening years, became the decisive reference. He would remain faithful to this spirit in the future, although he would have to reconcile it with his ever-present rebellious tendencies. Indeed, he would have recourse to organized violence that is rooted in his first readings and dreams of heroism, but which, at least in the hardened, institutionalized form he would give it in the thirties, was a far cry from the kind of politics he was envisioning at this point.

In 1920, Mao identified with the communist mode, all the while remaining an advocate of Chinese-style activism and a Chinese civil society; i.e. a provincial and sparse one, forced to forge links with reformist notables and navigate the dangerous straits between militarist factions. In Shanghai, the leaders of the Communist Party in the 1920s would have some difficulty reconciling their vision of a modern revolution with the reality of China's disintegration following the collapse of the Empire: in the political and military spheres, but also in the growing gap between the growth and Westernization of urban, "Blue" China and the countryside, underdeveloped and archaic by comparison.

This factor was decisive in Mao's initial political orientation, and also in his transition from activist to guerrilla leader, and finally, to national power.

*A*fter the May 4th Movement, studying abroad was all the rage. France succeeds Japan—land of education and exile of the preceding generation—as the beacon of modernity. The young men and women who did go didn't necessarily follow the political itinerary of Zhou Enlai or Deng Xiaoping, two famous "alumni" of France. Other students went to Moscow with the intention of initiating themselves to communism, like Liu Shaoqi. Subsequently, the Sun Yat-sen University of Moscow would train numerous officials of the Chinese Communist Party, and of the Guomindang.
Ph © L'Illustration/Sygma

Chapter 3

THE **P**OLITICS OF **O**THERS

19**21**–19**27**

IN 1923, MOSCOW SUMMONED CHINESE COMMUNISTS TO JOIN WITH SUN YAT-SEN'S GUOMINDANG. IT WAS MAO'S FIRST OPPORTUNITY TO RISE TO PROMINENCE, AND TO CONFIRM HIS BELIEF IN THE IMPORTANCE OF RURAL CHINA.

Both a rebel and a man of power, an activist and a politician, Mao Zedong had to resolve these contradictory aspects of his character in order to arrive at a synthesis that could be successful in the political arena. In the meantime, his activism was lodged in the politics of other prominent figures, and his own stature grew through opportunities well seized. From 1921 to 1927, Mao the provincial agitator had declared allegiance to the united front of the CCP and the Guomindang, but more as a Hunanese patriot and a disciple of Sun Yat-sen than as a militant communist. It was the crisis of 1927 that took him back to his country roots, and forced him to fashion his own political weapons.

In 1920, Tan Yankai returned to Changsha. Until 1927, Mao followed in the meandering wake of this typical representative of the provincial elite born out of the failed Republic with its militaristic tendencies and autonomist movement of Sun Yat-sen's local notables. Mao became the headmaster of a small offshoot of the Normal School 1, which was a step up on the social ladder; he was no longer snubbed as a provincial or seen as the launderer's employee from Shanghai; he was the son-in-law of Professor Yang. His public activities put him in touch with the autonomists. Somewhere from Mao's burgeoning web of social and political connections, emerged a Hunan-style communist.

Contrary to legend, which regards Mao as the founder and leader of Hunanese communism, it was He Minfan

*After the insurrection of March 22, 1927 the workers' militias of Shanghai spearheaded a deceptive victory, which Chiang Kai-shek undermined on April 12th by turning on his communist allies. It was further limited by the lack of unity among the revolutionary formations, and the lack of coordination between the urban movements and the peasant insurgents. And yet, although the "flagship" city of Blue China was not the only epicenter of revolutionary ardor, it remained the symbol of the 1920s-China and the rise to prominence of both cities and urban workers in the new social and political landscape.
Ph © L'Illustration/Sygma*

Liu Shaoqi (1898–1969) "led" the Anyuan proletariat during the strike of 1922. Through his exploits as a labor agitator, he became an influential symbol of the urban workers' revolution, and wielded considerable power within the Communist Party as Mao's alter ego. Liu was excommunicated during the Cultural Revolution, and died in oblivion.
Painting by Hou Yi Min (1961).
Ph © Roger-Viollet

that the modest Changsha group gravitated to in September of 1920. The delegate who made the strongest impression at the Congress of July 1921 was neither Mao nor a Hunanese at all, but Zhang Guotao, a disciple of the Red Pavilion (Li Dazhao's group in Beijing) who was the head of the Shanghai secretariat that coordinated militant activity among the workers. Within the Red Pavilion, Zhang had been instrumental in imposing a worker-oriented strategy rather than an alliance with the Guomindang.

Hunanese Communism

Following his appointment as head of the Hunanese branch of the secretariat, Mao set out in search of workers, only to discover that, in Hunan as elsewhere, the anarchists were already well installed among a rather backward proletariat. Most workers were simply displaced peasants. Their insurrections were violent but short-lived, and they habitually let local notables decide their fate, for they supported their "patriotic" actions on behalf of the Province. The anarchists endeavored to free the workers from this dependent relationship—which Mao approved

of, while criticizing their rejection of politics. Finding more notables and intellectuals in Changsha than workers, at the end of 1921, Mao went to Anyuan, in neighboring Jiangxi Province. But it was Li Lisan, his deputy, and Liu Shaoqi upon his return from the USSR, who managed to organize a trade union, and along with it, the strike of 1922. This was not an easy task, for the local notables were ready to co-manage the operation with agitators adept at organizing with undisciplined workers.

The mines of Jiangxi. Linked to the Xiang River basin by a railroad, the Pingxiang and Anyuan mines employed thousands of workers; it was the proletarian center of central China. It was also a mine of workers for Communist Party envoys from the Hunan in 1921–22. Contrary to Mao, who only visited the area twice in 1921, Liu Shaoqi and Li Lisan would find their vocation as labor agitators.

While Liu and Li had honed their class struggle skills in Shanghai, Mao's experience with workers remained at an embryonic stage. He saw education as the way to mobilize the masses. He co-managed, with He Minfan, a cultural bookstore that served as a front for propaganda activities. He expressed his penchant for the provincial pedagogical tradition through a popular education program he called the University of the Self-Taught. Students could advance in their studies without losing touch with real life—just as Mao himself had done. Though Mao no longer rejected connections and money as he had in 1917, he remained faithful to his progressive ideals. It is significant, though, that his modus operandi, his "praxis" (a Marxist term that he would soon give much thought to), was far more that of a negotiator and agitator, who skillfully navigated the murky currents of Hunanese political life, than that of a die-hard internationalist intent on destroying the enemy through clandestine party action. To be sure, this model was generally more revered theoretically than practically; coordination within the national movements was weak, even in Shanghai. That is why those who held the reins of the Party—Chen Duxiu, Zhang Guotao, Cai Hesen, Li Lisan—criticized "particularism" and "provincialism." Mao was to remember this.

But the Party leaders quickly had to face a more serious crisis. Following the Second Komintern Congress of July 1920, Maring imposed the strategy, decided by the Congress, of an alliance with the Guomindang—an alliance they had rejected the previous year. Where Chinese communists saw a betrayal of their identity; Mao saw a precious opportunity. It validated his style of politics, and allowed him to climb the ladder within a party he thought better equipped than the Communist Party to mobilize and politicize the masses.

The First United Front and Mao's Rise to Power

The 1922 strikes seemed to vindicate a strategy centered upon the workers. Anyuan, with its 300 Communist Party members, was like a "little Moscow"; for an elitist party created by a few dozen intellectuals who all knew each other, this was a success! Unfortunately, the spell was soon broken by the militarist Wu Peifu's brutal repression of a railroad strike in February 1927. Maring took advantage of this dramatic circumstance to summon the most zealous of the communist converts to get along with Sun Yat-sen. At the same time, he put a stop to Moscow's confusion over whom to support—even Wu Peifu, the brutal warlord of the North, had been considered!

Sun himself had been evicted from Canton by a warlord, with whom he had governed the city since 1920. In January 1923, he signed an accord with Adolphe Joffé, the Soviet envoy, by which the USSR committed to helping the movement of national liberation without trying to force a communist-led solution. Under the aegis of General Blücher, alias Galen, and Borodin (see sidebar), weapons, funds, and advisers flowed into Canton, where Sun regained power in early 1923.

Master of Northern China, which he dominated until 1924, the warlord Wu Peifu (1874–1939) brutally repressed striking workers of the Beijing–Hakou railroad on February 7, 1923. He had pretended to encourage the strikers, in order to disorganize his adversary's communications.
Ph © Roger Pic

The Communists adhered individually to the Guomindang, reorganized according to the Soviet model. At Whampoa (Huangpo), near Canton, a military academy trained officers under the leadership of Chiang Kai-shek, to whom the graduates remained fiercely loyal. Zhou Enlai, back from Europe, was his political commissar.

One might ask why Moscow hadn't directly armed the Communists, instead of those that would crush them in 1927. The reason lies in the Soviets' perception of the

Chinese activists as a band of intellectuals mired in a dead-end obsession with the workers—what they called a "childhood illness." The issue would come to a head during the 1927 crisis; the military apparatus, led by Chiang Kai-shek, would turn out to be uncontrollable, while the Communist Party was transformed, primarily by its alliance with the Guomindang.

From the middle of the 1920s, the Communist Party opened its doors to a more massive recruitment of workers as well as intellectuals. With 58,000 militants in the spring of 1927 (half of whom were workers), it was the third largest in the world, after the Russian and the German parties. Firmly rooted in the trade unions, especially in Shanghai and Canton, it had adopted the Leninist formula, although its ideological base remained nationalistic. The May 30th Movement gave it a renewed impetus. At Shanghai, the police of the International Concession had fired upon demonstrators, sparking a cascade of protests by students, workers, and businessmen. Like the famous May 4th Movement, this one rapidly spread to other cities. In Canton, it lasted 16 months, although Beijing and the North were hardly affected. The Chinese Revolution was still in quest of its geography.

In March of the same year, the death of Sun Yat-sen led to a war of succession within the Guomindang. Chiang Kai-shek triumphed over rivals to the right (Hu Hanmin) and to the left (Wang Jingwei) in Canton, with the benediction of the Soviets—with whom he would break in a decisive coup de force on March 20, 1926. Communist Party leaders were determined to recover their independence, and Borodin and the Russian communists reluctantly withdrew. At Canton, Mao Zedong, Guomindang official, communist at heart but on an extended sabbatical from the Party, was not unduly concerned.

Chiang Kai-shek was certainly not a Zeng Guofan, that is, the ideal incarnation of the warrior-statesman Mao venerated. Mao's own path to prominence was far more ambiguous, marked by stubborness, frustration, and ambition. In 1923, partisans of a United Front were so scarce that his commitment won him a seat on the Central Committee, where he succeeded Zhang Guotao as coordinator. But he clearly

Mikhail Marcovitch Güsenberg, alias Borodin (1884–1951), secret agent of the Komintern in Latin America, was sent to the Chinese front in 1923. He was convinced that the Chinese Communist Party could only be the beast of burden of the Revolution, and he kept the first United CP-Guomindang Front at arm's length. Chiang Kai-shek would be less intimidated than Sun Yat-sen.
Ph © Roger-Viollet

THE CANTON BASE

Most of the May 4th activists believed, like Mao, that a united Guomindang-CP was the dream of 1919 of a "great union" come true. In spite of its lack of cohesion, Sun Yat-sen's party created a truly national political arena within a fragmented nation, and a bridge between rural Yellow and urban Blue China. The effects were initially positive in Canton, but the communists would suffer a humiliating defeat by Chiang Kai-shek on April 12, 1927, causing them to bitterly regret the alliance. Ulterior motives not withstanding, the partners learned to work together. Sun Yat-sen praised and made use of the communist propensity to organize the popular base he was determined to give his party. The Guomindang finally acquired the firm structure that it had been lacking. But these convergences do not mean that he made concessions to communism, even though he revised his 1914 program in a much more authoritarian direction. In his view, before achieving democracy it was necessary to recover the borders of the former Empire through a great offensive, dubbed the Northern Expedition, and then to govern the country with a firm hand. Reforms would be implemented through a dictatorship, what the Guomindang called a "tutelage." The communists were less enthusiastic about the alliance, above all the Central Committee, which remained in Shanghai. In Moscow, the Trotskites, opposed to the Front, considered the Guomindang to be an inherently bourgeois party, inclined to treachery, and Chiang an inevitable Bonaparte. But Stalin and Bukharin, who had sidelined Trotsky after Lenin's death in 1924, saw the Guomindang as a cross-section of classes, enriched by communism: a nationalist bourgeoisie, a petite bourgeoisie, workers, and peasants. The unity of these four classes was attributable to the "semi-feudal" nature of Chinese society.

These theoretical considerations were perhaps less important than the realistic perception of the political and military situation: the proletariat and the intellectuals were too weak by themselves to carry out a Russian-style revolution. As for the Party, Karl Radek mocked its Confucianist soul-searching at the Fourth Komintern Congress in December 1922, in the very presence of Chen Duxiu! The social dynamic was not at the right stage for a transition to socialism, in the Komintern view, and in the meantime, priority was to be given to mobilizing the masses around nationalism and agrarian reform. From 1924–25, it was to be the United Guomindang-PC Front's mission to give political form to this directive. ■

Bukharin and Stalin in the 1920s.
Ph © Coll. Viollet

did not belong to the Maring clique, nor to the restricted circle of "great" intellectuals who were establishing the Front's theoretical foundations by analyzing rural and urban society (Chen Duxiu) and the historical particularities of Chinese capitalism (Qu Qiubai, a former Red Pavilion member, was recently back from the USSR). Behind the alliance with Sun Yat-sen a vision of China both more orthodox and more open to the rural heart of the country was evolving—but Mao agreed neither with it nor with the Front's foes, such as Peng Shuzhi, whose view put the proletariat at the head of the Revolution. Mao glorified the bourgeoisie. In the summer of 1923, he praised the revolt of the Shanghai chamber of commerce, which declared independence following one of the many politico-military upheavals in the city. That year, the dogmatic stance of the Party kept him sidelined and in retreat. He was even more marginalized in 1924, when Maring departed, and Peng Shuzhi returned from the USSR. With Chen Duxiu hesitating, the Front was once again in question.

No longer finding the Communist Party hospitable to his ambitions, Mao pursued his rise within a reorganized Guomindang. Elected to the Central Executive Commission (CEC), he was then sent to the Shanghai Party Bureau, where he worked for Hu Hanmin. The year 1924 marked his first true entry into "national" politics, at the risk of seeming a Guomindang right-wing Nationalist (of which Hu Hanmin was one of the most prominent). Li Lisan, another of the Front's adversaries, derided him, calling him "Hu's secretary." Illness—or perhaps an identity crisis— prompted Mao to return to his native Shaoshan for a few months. At the Fourth Congress of the Communist Party in 1925, he was excluded from the CEC; within the Guomindang, he remained a bystander to the internal power struggles from which Chiang Kai-shek would emerge victorious in 1926. The momentum of the May 4th Movement had produced an enthusiastic,

With the army behind him, Chiang Kai-shek (1887–1975) was in a position to arbitrate between the factions at Sun Yat-sen's death in 1925. On March 20th 1926, he quelled the trade unions' influence, and that of the "soviet councilors" of Canton. At the launch of the Northern Expedition in July, he was Commander in Chief of the Nationalist armies.
Ph © Coll. Viollet

Li Lisan (1899–1967) was one of the most important workers' syndicate leaders in Shanghai in the 1920s. A Hunanese and an alumnus of the same school as Mao, Cai Hesen, and Liu Shaoqi, he always kept his distance from Mao, personally and politically. The Red Guards would not forgive him, executing him in 1967 at the height of the Cultural Revolution.

Ph © Edimédia

activist Mao; in the aftermath of the May 30th Movement, he was indifferent, on leave from his party and from politics in general. Official history has left this period and the winding path Mao took to get there, unexamined, mentioning only the significant fact that, in the second half of 1925, Mao did some "agit-prop" in the villages around Shaoshan.

The Peasant's Path

Mao Zedong's affair with the peasants was not a sudden or original illumination; he simply took up a movement that had been abandoned by its first pioneers. Following the Komintern's leaders, the Chinese Communist Party shifted its emphasis to the historically agrarian roots of the country. Of course, the peasantry was not in and of itself a viable revolutionary force; for partisans of the Front, it was the role of the bourgeoisie (or of the proletariat, for its opponents) to resolve the "peasant question." Peng Pai was an isolated example until 1924, when the peasantry's visibility and influence started to grow. In Moscow, Bukharin was elaborating a vision of communism that played out the war between the bourgeoisie and the proletariat on a planetary scale, with peasant mobilization as the key to victory. The

peasantry, in his view, was concentrated at the periphery of the industrialized West, among the colonized peoples of Asia. For Bukharin, and for Mao later, the "proletarian path" necessitated controlling the "world village," organizing its masses as a whole, and overriding divisions within it. Proponents of Bukharin's doctrine recommended tapping mid-level farmers and also those who had been demoted (déclassé) as a possible revolutionary source. This was a far cry from Lenin's taboo against any form of communist action in the countryside; precise and concrete actions were being planned to mobilize the villages. The "peasant question" had become a rural strategy.

In China, Peng Pai's example was relayed by Yun Daiying (1895–executed in 1931). A former peasant activist, proponent of educational activism, he converted to urban communism as he moved from Sichuan to Hubei then to Shanghai. In 1924–25, Yun exhorted readers of his weekly *Communist Youth* to return to the countryside—where most of his readers came from—in order to develop their character through contact with the peasants, and sow the seeds of revolution. Simply talking about Marx in the villages would only produce wariness or indifference: one had to take an interest in their daily lives, and win their confidence by proposing concrete solutions to their problems. Politicizing the peasants entailed competing against traditional power structures already in place. But this was the goal—to conquer every village—and the key to victory in this class struggle, or so went the theory, which Mao would considerably amplify.

Mao's rural conversion was not really a departure. After all, the Guomindang was the "secular" arm of the Communist Party in the countryside. A Rural Department had been created in 1924, at the same time as Peng Pai was named director of a new Training Institute for rural militants. While officially recognized, the circle of activists involved in rural strategy remained small: Peng Pai's Institute had only 800 graduates, while the Whampoa Military Academy turned out over 8,000 officers. At any rate, Mao joined Peng in late 1925 when, evicted from the Hunan, he returned to Canton. From May to October 1926, he was director of the Training

The exception confirms the rule: Peng Pai (1896–executed in 1929). A Guangdong Communist, born in Haifeng Prefecture (east of Canton), he organized a peasant association there in 1922. He was one of the few that converted to communism after May 4th who attempted to directly implement a soviet model of organization without having recourse to worker agitation.
Ph © Archives CDCC

Institute's sixth graduating class. His teachings and writings often mention the downtrodden elements of rural society— soldiers, bandits, beggars, wanderers, prostitutes—and secret societies, references that some have attributed to Mao's penchant for romantic novels. But the logic behind this rather un-Marxist thinking, however, was that of Bukharin, whose collected works were available in translation at the Institute. Mao prefaced one of the volumes, with the benediction of Qu Qiubai, who was the main representative of Bukharin's thought in China. Although Mao's reading, characteristically rustic and Chinese, lacked the subtlety of Qu's, the two men faced the disintegration of the United Front from the same point of view.

The Disintegration of the United Front

Chiang Kai-shek's Northern Expedition, facilitated by the rallying of many southern militarists, reached the Yangtze in the fall of 1926, then Nanking and Shanghai in the spring of the following year. In the central provinces of Hunan and Hubei, the peasants took advantage of the power vacuum to revolt. Peasant associations mushroomed, and land was confiscated. These rapid developments provoked a dramatic political crisis. The two forces in play—the army and the peasants—would from this point until 1949 dominate the Chinese Revolution; for the moment, they put the United Front in serious jeopardy. The Communists had no more control over the one than the other; unable to bring the two together, they didn't win over the generals after dropping the strategy of alliance with the peasants in June 1927. This crisis was in a way the reverse of the situation twenty years later, when Mao would succeed in unifying peasants and armed forces.

While Trotsky and some Chinese communists judged the Front to be condemned by a "militarist cancer," Stalin and Bukharin held to their 1923–24 analysis. Military might was more potent than the social dynamic, still mired in particularism despite appearances to the contrary. A global victory by the Guomindang sounded more promising than limited successes (such as the scattered implementation of Trotsky's system of

A document from the peasant association of Lufeng, near Haifeng, cradle of rural communism since Peng Pai (June 15, 1926)
Ph © Archives CDCC

A common misperception places Mao Zedong at the head of a Chinese tradition of Marxist-Leninist class theory. His analysis of the peasant classes and their attitudes toward the Revolution published in 1926 drew heavily on Chen Duxiu's and Qu Qiubai's economic and historical analysis of class structure (1923). In the context of the "pact with the devil' (the Guomindang), they had had to rethink the Revolution, and found that China's special situation was potentially favorable to new alliances. In this respect, they used orthodox methods to come to an unorthodox conclusion, at least from the Marxist point of view: if the Chinese people were divided socially and economically, they were essentially united politically. Mao's New Democracy of the 1940s would make ample usage of this, and more generally of the style of class analysis imparted by the follows of Bukharin in the 1920s, of which his 1926 study is a prime example:

"Go into the countryside, go anywhere. It suffices to observe attentively to determine that there are eight different categories of people: the great landowners, the small landowners, landed peasants, semi-landed peasants, sharecroppers, poor peasants, peasant laborers and artisans, and the déclassés, or excluded elements. These eight

categories are eight distinct classes, whose very different economic status and lifestyle leads to different psychological compositions that entail different attitudes toward the Revolution. [...] The landed peasants belong to the petite bourgeoisie. There are three different types of landed peasants. [...] In peacetime, the attitudes of these three types [...] toward the Chinese Revolution are all different. But in a period [...] of revolutionary fervor [...], not only will the third type of landed peasants, with left-wing tendencies, immediately participate in the Revolution, but the second, neutral type too, has the potential to participate. Even the first type, the right-leaning landed peasants [...], must inevitably join the Revolution. [...]"

[After describing at length the peasant case, Mao turns to the ostracized segments of Chinese society.]

"Among their number are soldiers, bandits, beggars, and prostitutes. [...] These people are capable of great bravery; led with justice, they can become a revolutionary force. [...] Under no circumstances must they be forced to go over to the enemy as a counter-revolutionary force.
As for the great landowners, the tactic must be combative, for they must be forced to make political and economic concessions. In certain cases, when [...] one encounters particularly zealous counter-

revolutionary elements, who are wicked and exploit the people, then these people must be eliminated."

(Extract from *Mao Tse-toung* by Stuart Schram. Armand Colin, Paris, 1963.)

Besides this first concrete and unifying portrayal of the peasantry, another thematic constant was emerging at this early stage: Mao was concerned with political efficiency. This is evident in the moral terms in which he couches his analyses, bypassing and competing directly with economically based classifications, which enabled him, in short, to be inclusive. The last two categories—small landowners and the ostracized segments—were considered by Mao to be the pillars of rural society, and he would reassert their importance in his 1930s assaults on the Party dogma of "class against class." ∎

An old dream of Sun Yat-sen, the Northern Expedition against the warlords was politically quagmired in 1927, following a string of victories the previous year. Militarily, it culminated in Chiang's taking of Beijing in June 1928. Chiang had temporarily sidelined the communists, but he was surrounded by rivals and allies; this mitigated his victory over the warlords.

Soviets), so the decision was taken to maintain the Front and to obtain popular support for this priority. The Seventh Komintern Congress of November 1926 renewed the alliance with Chiang Kai-shek's party, while criticizing his anti-peasant policies, and calling for the implementation of his moderate program of agrarian reform. On the terrain, however, the Komintern's "armchair scenario" left the actors tepid; one by one, they left the stage—except for the communists and the workers' militia of Shanghai, caught up in a general strike on March 22, 1927. On Moscow's orders, Chiang Kai-shek was put in command of Shanghai, and the militias disarmed. The night of April 12, Chiang's and other henchmen took control of the key points of the city in a violent raid. Territory under Chiang was "normalized"; in Nanking, an anti-communist government was installed.

Moscow had overestimated its capacity to "squeeze

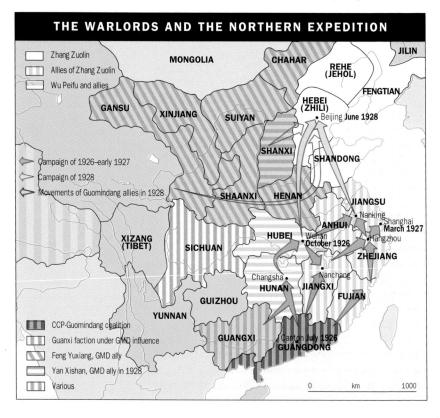

THE WARLORDS AND THE NORTHERN EXPEDITION

Zhang Zuolin
Allies of Zhang Zuolin
Wu Peifu and allies

Campaign of 1926–early 1927
Campaign of 1928
Movements of Guomindang allies in 1928

CCP-Guomindang coalition
Guanxi faction under GMD influence
Feng Yuxiang, GMD ally
Yan Xishan, GMD ally in 1928
Various

MONGOLIA CHAHAR REHE (JEHOL) JILIN
FENGTIAN
GANSU XINJIANG SUIYAN HEBEI (ZHILI) • Beijing June 1928
SHANXI SHANDONG
SHAANXI HENAN JIANGSU
  • Nanking
ANHUI • Shanghai March 1927
XIZANG (TIBET) SICHUAN HUBEI Wuhan October 1926 Hangzhou
ZHEJIANG
Changsha • Nanchang •
HUNAN JIANGXI FUJIAN
GUIZHOU
YUNNAN
GUANGXI Canton July 1926
GUANGDONG

0   km   1000

the lemon," in Stalin's words, through the subtle dose of social concessions and political pressure that had been Borodin's work. Intent on having his revenge after Chiang's takeover of the Guomindang on March 20, 1926, he put the communists back in the saddle by organizing a mixed (CP-Guomindang) government at Hanku, backed by Hunan and Hubei militarists opposed to Chiang. Pending the return of Wang Jingwei (exiled in France), Tan Yankai ran this government that took over from the Front on April 12. In the shadow of his mentor, Mao joined the Directorate of Peasant Associations, whose mission was to redefine agricultural policy for the anti-Chiang coalition. He thus found himself at the center of a contradiction that would split the Wuhan Front wide open in July.

After failed offensives in October 1926 and February 1927, the Communists won a fragile victory against the warlord of Shanghai on March 22. Real power was in the hands of merchants, notables, foreigners, secret societies, and arms traffickers, and Chiang Kai-shek brought them all into his crushing assault against the Communists on April 12th. The French novelist André Malraux recounted these murky events in his famous novel, The Human Condition.
Ph © Edimédia

A Difficult Spring: 1927

Although the peasants had not revolted throughout China, they were sufficiently active in Hunan and Hubei Provinces to undermine the agrarian compromise encouraged by the Soviets. In the spring of 1927, Moscow seemed to backpedal in their favor. With Chiang out of the picture as far as friendship with the Communists was concerned, Bukharin responded to critics of the Front by reasserting its activist foundation. The Communist Party was to exert pressure on the Guomindang by playing off civilians against officers, left against right—and provoke the masses to take

Mao entered politics on the wave of the May 4th Movement, in the pacific and consensual spirit of the United Front. In 1927, peasant unrest revealed a more violent dimension, hardening his conception of the class struggle through this particularly Chinese deviation— the peasantry was no proletariat.
Ph © Roger Pic

action against the institutional apparatus. This strategy aimed to exploit the political contradictions of the Guomindang in order to achieve room for trade unions and peasant associations to maneuver. Keeping a hand on the reins of the social movements, Bukharin facilitated an evolution toward the left. The choice between the Guomindang and the masses as chief ally was no longer the order of the day. From one point of view, the Communists were just getting by, making the best of defeat. But Bukharin was not Stalin, and did not see everything through the lens of power.

In this spirit, Qu Qiubai relayed Bukharin's directives. Opposed both to Borodin's pragmatic concessions and to the desire, widespread among his colleagues in the CEC (Chen Duxiu and Peng Shuzhi indirectly, and Zhang Guotao and Li Lisan openly) to break with the Front, Qu Qiubai emphasized rigorous leadership of the masses— especially the peasants—within a reactivated Front. He recognized the importance of social dynamics and sought to use these forces. Mao shared this vision. Many historians have been troubled by Mao's seeming contradictory status in politics in early 1927, and his double allegiance. Amid considerable debate, the Peasants' Association of China and the government's agrarian policy endeavored to find a compromise with forces hostile to the peasant revolution. Mao personally conducted an inquiry into the unstable districts of northern Changsha in the winter of 1926–27; this tour confirmed his faith in the strength and the historical role of the peasants.

Indeed, his Report on an Investigation of the Peasant Movement in Hunan exalted the peasants' strength to the point of exaggeration: they were arming themselves, organizing, struggling—the Hunan was all but theirs. This was far from the case. But Mao tapped into the voluntarist vein he had already exploited in his writings of 1919; except that by 1927 the issues of violence and the conquest of power had given his thought a new twist. What had been obtained in terms of political concessions became a pretext for much more radical demands. Mao saw great potential in the raw power of the peasant masses, although his report provides no concrete plan of action. What Mao did explicitly was to ask the question: "Who are our enemies? Who are our friends?" Many commentators have read into this a desire to break with the political customs of the 1920s, and with the Guomindang, which happened at the end of the year.

Less obvious to us today than it was to Mao and his report's audience was that party structure had become a crucial issue. Mao never entertained the idea of leaving his official post, for the simple reason that, in spite of his emphasis on the peasantry, he knew that an organized party was necessary to achieve power. The report makes no mention of this because there was little political structure within the peasant movements to describe. Mao's voluntarism bore a profound affinity to Bukharin, in the sense that they both recognized that, to save China, the revolution had to be taken to the national level. Outside his report, Mao admitted that it would take several Hunans to render the Party useless. The choice of sides in the Front was therefore not whether or not to remain with the Guomindang, but to decide with which Guomindang the Communists were to remain; in other words, to take power within the Guomindang. This report was an important stage in Mao's self-assertion, for the ambiguities that it implicitly referred to when one knew

The Revolution is not a banquet between distinguished people.... It is an uprising, an act of violence by which one class overthrows another.

Report on an Investigation of the Peasant Movement in the Hunan, 1927.

his political character. As we have seen, the apparent contradictions were evidence of his profound realism— unfortunately, his vision was premature, and the situation not as ripe as he would have wished. Nevertheless, with Qu Qiubai's preface, the report was published by the Communists. The Komintern newspaper gave it an interested review, and Bukharin had yet more material to justify the Soviets' keeping their bet on the CCP.

On the ground, the absence of coordination rendered the peasant movement chaotic. The Party had neither the time nor the means to mobilize and control the masses, and even less, to influence the military or the Guomindang. On May 21, repression loomed ominously around Changsha. Mao called for caution and patience. The Front survived until mid-July, followed by a wave of insurrections; encouraged by Moscow, the Communists did their best to reconquer the "revolutionary base." But they came out shattered, with a few thousand survivors hiding in Shanghai, and the countryside. At year's end, alienated from both the CCP and the Guomindang, Mao was one of those who renounced insurrections to take up guerrilla warfare. The tensions of the spring had erupted, and the CCP had proved itself as incapable as the Guomindang of mobilizing the

masses—that was the hard lesson of 1927.

Mao remained faithful to the idea of running the Revolution politically, but he had reached the end of the road in terms of relying on the politics of others. Rather than base his activism on politics, he would now make politics subservient to activism. By forcing him to redefine his political stance far from the urban and national horizon of the twenties, the rupture of 1927 would bring Mao closer to the most radical elements of rebellion, cutting him off from all hopes of leadership within the Communist Party, as well as from an imperial vision, which he would never renounce. A new and much more difficult epoch of tension was to come, and would be resolved only by the Japanese invasion and the Long March.

Stricken in Shanghai in April 1927, the urban dream of the Communists was shattered in July in Wuhan. The capital of Hubei Province was made up of the three cities of Wuchang, Hanyang, and Hanku—whose ruins are shown below (1911). In 1938, the winds of fortune would again buffet Wuhan, when Wang Ming attempted against Mao's wishes to create a new urban base for the CCP—taking advantage of the Japanese invasion and the Second United Front...
Ph © Edimédia

Chapter 4

THE **R**EBEL

19**28**–19**35**

Having renounced urban communism after the disintegration of the First United Front, Mao lost control of the Jiangxi guerilla troops in 1933. The Long March then turned the tables in his favor.

P receded by a short-lived coup in Nanchang (August 1, 1927), the Autumn Harvest Uprising was a disaster for the Chinese Communists, but a break for Mao Zedong. While the pro-Communist officers of Nanchang (among them Zhu De) were retreating in a proto-Long March, Lominadze, the new "eye" of Moscow, laid the blame on Chen Duxiu for the defeat. Moscow's impeccable strategy had been undermined by a form of "right-wing opportunism." As a result, opposition figures within the CCP were rewarded, in particular the followers of Bukharin. Thus Qu Qiubai succeeded Chen, and Mao entered the Politburo as a substitute member (August 7).

New insurrections broke out in Hubei and in Hunan, where the Party had concentrated most of its forces. The objective was to take Changsha by fomenting revolt in the surrounding villages during the tense period after the harvest when landlords and farmers settle their accounts. But when the commander of one of the Hunanese "Committees of the Front" Mao, who was then captured by the local police, battalions defected, and the peasants stood still. The attack on Changsha planned for September 16 had to be cancelled. On the 19th, after coming within minutes of being shot by a firing squad, Mao escaped and fled with others to Jiangxi. Instead of returning to Changsha, they headed toward the Jinggang Mountains, which separate the two southern provinces.

Mao in 1933: a rebel among rebels, at age forty he was reduced to the status of a bystander in the Communist leadership. By the following year, the situation turns round to his favor...
Ph © Coll. J.A.F./Magnum

Meanwhile, Mao had been expelled from the politburo for his military adventures. Qu wanted to open a major rural front without abandoning the urban front; in his opinion, Mao and others criticized by the Party had deserted. The Soviets distanced themselves from Qu's putschism, without giving up on their vision of an urban-centered revolution, or on rural recognition for that matter. When, to counter Trotsky, Stalin saw fit to approve the formation of Soviets (in September), his objective was still focused on the southern cities. Peng Pai proclaimed the first Chinese Soviet in November; his reign was violent and brief. Canton was the prize in December, and Qu Qiubai bore the responsibility for the failed Commune and brutal repression. At the Sixth Congress of the CCP (summer 1928) a new team, dominated by Li Lisan, replaced him.

The climax of the armed insurrections of 1927 took place in Canton. The brutal repression of December convinced Mao of the futility of attacking the enemy where it was strongest. He did want to "force history," but not that way.
Ph © L'Illustration/Sygma

Maoism's Debut

Far from the struggles of Shanghai and Moscow, the guerrillas were re-enacting *Water Margin* and *The Three Kingdoms* at the distant reaches of the Hunan, Jiangxi, Hubei, and even Northern China. Delving ever deeper into the mountains and the swamps of the periphery, they followed the movements of the enemy: "If he advances, we retreat; if he retreats, we advance." They raided poorly defended villages and left them as soon

as they had found weapons and ammunition. As Mao himself had lucidly observed, if the masses remained "cold and distant," it would become necessary to form alliances with figures of the underworld—local warlords, criminals, and secret societies. The Guomindang state, established after the taking of Beijing in 1928, was torn by internecine strife; Mao, as a CCP official, sought within this context other reasons for "Red Power" to exist.

Bandits and secret societies were legendary in the Jinggangshan region. The guerrillas' improvised alliances with outcasts enraged the Hunan Central Committee, which accused them of rampant militarism. Mao led his own guerrilla front from within the Party, while remaining loyal to its leaders; his rebellious spirit did not extend to creating a new party... until the Cultural Revolution of the sixties. In the spring of 1928, the plan was to attack from the south of Hunan, after a rendezvous with the escapees of Nanchang, led by Zhu De. Peng Dehuai, a native of Xiangtang who had led a revolt in Pingjiang (Hunan) in July, arrived on the scene in November. With Peng in charge of guarding the Jinggangshan, Mao and Zhu forced their way across the Jiangxi, reaching the mountainous border of Fujian. Peng joined them in 1929, adding his 800 men to the 2,000 Hunanese.

The Communists left behind them agricultural reforms as violent as Peng Pai's had been, imposed from the top down, just like in Haifeng. From this new base in Jiangxi/Fujian, Mao set out to win the people's acceptance of communist domination by politicizing them, not neglecting the army or the Party itself. This thoroughness would be one of the hallmarks of Mao's political way.

Mao made abundant use of the terrain, which he acquired a precise knowledge of through exhaustive surveys. "Didactic operations" were carried out with the aim of defining, and inverting the power relationship in the villages. In line with the approach he had developed in 1926–7, Mao pinpointed the crucial areas of political opportunity within the rural power structure. Contrary to Moscow's doctrine (and Shanghai's) of "class against class," Mao included small landowners and even some rich peasants in his "front of the masses," to fight against a designated group of "exploiters." Of course,

Qu Qiubai (1899–1935), the favorite of Maring and Borodin, succeeded Chen Duxiu at the head of the Party, only to fall into disgrace for his aggressive militarism. A great intellectual from the lower Yangtze region, he was initiated to communism in Moscow. More than Mao or his Hunanese classmates, he incarnated the elite of communism in the 1920s. He was captured in Jiangxi at the beginning of the Long March, and shot in 1935.
Ph © Archives CDCC

the Communists had to prove that they were able to defend not only the peasants, but also the rural elite itself, for the exploiters were also the protectors of the people, and their intermediary with the outside world. Rural hegemony would be more easily achieved with their help—not that Mao had any intention of abandoning terror as a means of control. From the start, Mao "walked on two legs." From the initial efforts at mobilization and the demonstrations of force, an association of impoverished peasants crystallized, as well as a core group of activists who would later join the CCP or the army.

THE JINGGANG MOUNTAINS

Lake Dongting

Nanchang ■

Changsha ■   •Pingxiang

Xiangtan•

HUNAN *Jinggang Mountains*

Xiang River *(Jinggangshan)*   **JIANGXI**

Gan River

0   km   150

GUANGDONG

Zhu De and Agnes Smedley at the end of the Long March (1936). Older than Mao, Zhu De, like Deng Xiaoping, was a native of Sichuan. A soldier since childhood, he had been an officer in the 4th Nationalist Army. In tribute to this, the army Zhu and Mao assembled in Jinggangshan in 1928 was dubbed the 4th Red Army.
Ph © H. Snow/Magnum

Agrarian reform was but one aspect of Mao Zedong's ambitions. But other goals, such as emancipating women through marriage reform and doing away with ancestor worship, clan-oriented rituals, and Taoist sects, met with greater resistance. Mobilization could be spread too thin, ideologically; already, the guerrillas' constant movements made it difficult to maintain control over a fluid situation. Mao's strategy was called contradictory by many, but this was Maoism in the making: agrarian reform and mobilization were two perpetual struggles. The masses had to be educated and the revolution kept on the move at the same time. A sedentary revolution was against Mao's guerrilla ethos, which proclaimed a deep distrust of institutions and the devitalizing effects of government. Mao Zedong wanted his militants to retain their activist fiber, in this profound reversal of revolution, with politics taking priority over power itself.

Militants as well as the masses had to be mobilized and educated. Against arrogance and inertia, Mao Zedong prescribed political education, not in order to diminish their authority, but to "perfect their methods." The new ambition of the Chinese Communists, improving on Bukharin's model of 1926–7, was to implement the activist ideal of transforming and guiding a people who

THE VILLAGE POWER STRUCTURE

Against the official interpretation, many observers have tried to explain the Maoist Revolution as the result of increased poverty in the countryside: ever more farmers, high rents, and debt. And yet, the concentration of land was but one aspect of a complex tableau. Domains—not very large—were divided up into minuscule lots. At the bottom of the ladder, small landowners and sharecroppers lived side by side. Owning the land, or even renting it, was everyone's dream, for it meant a guarantee of survival. Rents were high: out of every four farmers, two would give the landlord between a third and half their harvest, one would

give more than half, and the last less than a third. Many were heavily indebted. Many small landowners or farmers lost their land and joined the fringes of society, but at the other end of the spectrum, concentration of land did not increase. This process of impoverishment was not really driven by capitalism. It was rather the result of a demographic explosion. Economic progress remained confined to the main cities and their environs. As for the rural elite, their influence increased as their activities diversified: trade in grain and money-lending, for example. They were the decision-makers at the local level, simultaneously exploiting and protecting the population. In

the vacuum left by a powerless government, landowners and chiefs became important intermediaries, and they disposed of organized militias to keep their enemies—bandits, tax-collectors, soldiers—at bay. This complex web of solidarity blurred the outlines of the classes, but the very ambivalence of the power relationships offered numerous opportunities for activist infiltration. In his "Report of Xunwu" (1930), Mao dissected the political and economic roots of this original landscape that fascinated him far more than debates about Marxist concepts. ■

LAND DISTRIBUTION, 1930–40			
	HOUSEHOLDS (%)	LAND (%)	AVERAGE AREA (ha)
LANDOWNERS AND RICH PEASANTS	approx 10	40–50	+2
INDEPENDENT PEASANTS	approx 30	50–60	0.7 to 2
SMALL LANDOWNERS (POOR PEASANTS)	approx 60		0.7 and less

Mao's first wife, Yang Kaihui, was executed in 1930 in reprisal against an offensive ordered by Li Lisan. Mao married the professor's daughter in defiance of his parents, who had arranged for him to marry a peasant girl. Her tragic end illustrates the extreme violence of the civil war between the CCP and the Guomindang. Two of Mao's brothers, and a sister, would perish in the Revolution; and Cai Hesen would be executed in 1931.
Ph © Roger Pic

were too reticent to take action on their own—and this included militants too. Education as an ideological tool was becoming one of Mao's main functions of power, prefiguring the re-education campaigns of later on. It was certainly not making the guerrillas into "super-democrats" opposed to the orthodox Shanghai Communists. His personal style, it might be added, had little to do with democracy, but rather with being anchored in the reality of the moment, with policies tailored to the situation. "No evidence, no right to speech" as he put it laconically in his article "Against Worship of Books" (1930). He cared little about Marxist concepts and the elegant formulations of his Shanghai or Moscow counterparts, "armchair revolutionaries" for whom he had little esteem. On the contrary, Mao's everyday voice rang out in Jiangxi as profoundly Chinese, and appealing to common sense. The practical solutions he proposed, however, were subordinated to an inflexible will.

The "Frog at the Bottom of the Well"

Mao's way was soon to bring him into direct conflict with the leaders of the CCP, and with other guerrilla chiefs who did not share his views. At first, he benefited from favorable circumstances. Chiang Kai-shek was too busy quelling his rivals to pay much attention to the Red bases, which were expanding and steadily gaining control of the villages. In early 1930, he was beleaguered, and revolutionary hopes ran high in Moscow, Jiangxi, but especially in Shanghai. Li Lisan readied his forces for the reconquest of central China. While troops north of the Yangtze failed to take Wuhan, Peng Dehuai occupied Changsha for ten days in late July. Zhu and a reluctant Mao launched a 24-hour assault on Nanchang on the first of August. Li again attacked Changsha, and Zhu and Mao received orders to meet Peng's army there. On August 13, they relinquished their position and headed for Jiangxi.

The fiasco of "Li Lisan's line" had more serious consequences in Shanghai. Stalin sent his adviser on Chinese affairs, Pavel Mif, to make a decision. The directorate was given to Zhou Enlai, and other posts to his protégés from Sun Yat-sen University. Wang Ming was the leader of the Bolshevik faction, 28 members strong, with Zhang Wentian and Qin Bang-Xian. But internecine strife and treachery undermined their secrecy. Leaving in Shanghai a "Bureau of White Affairs" headed by Liu Shaoqi, Wang Ming left for Moscow. Other leaders took refuge in the Soviet of Jiangxi-Fujian, where Mao had consolidated his power.

Taking advantage of the brutal combats in Shanghai, Mao Zedong drowned in blood a rebellion from within: those of his own militants and officers who were hostile to his line were falsely branded as faithful to Li Lisan and eliminated. Where politics failed, there was always the rule of force. Shanghai had no monopoly on repression and shady secret police; several of the police chiefs of the regime, such as the infamous Kang Sheng (a Moscow alumnus), completed their sinister

After Manchuria (1931), Shanghai (January 1932): the Japanese aggression would change the political and strategic situation in Jiangxi. Initially, to Mao's disfavor, his opponents' plan for attacking Chiang Kai-shek from the rear in a massive offensive seemed more attractive than prolonged guerilla warfare.
Ph © L'Illustration/Sygma

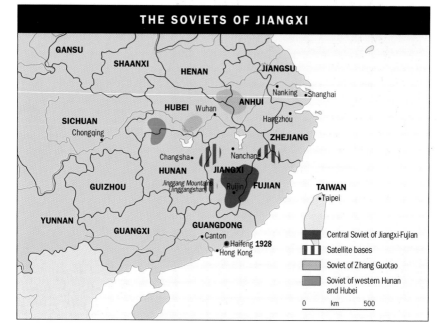

THE SOVIETS OF JIANGXI

Central Soviet of Jiangxi-Fujian

Satellite bases

Soviet of Zhang Guotao

Soviet of western Hunan and Hubei

0   km   500

Besides the Jiangxi/Fujian base and its satellites (including those of Jinggangshan), Zhang Guotao's base north of Yangtze represented the most important center of communist guerrilla warfare and, because of its proximity with Wuhan and Nanking, the most menacing for Chiang Kai-shek, who made it a priority to eliminate it.

apprenticeships in Jiangxi.

Meanwhile, Mao had repelled two offensives that Chiang Kai-shek, victorious over his rivals, had launched in response to Li Lisan's attacks. On his third attempt, he sent out his best divisions, and adapted to guerrilla tactics. The outcome was uncertain when the Japanese invaded Manchuria (September 1931). Mao quickly exploited the situation to his advantage. The Congress of Chinese Soviets that Li Lisan wanted to convene in Wuhan met in Rujin, capital of Jiangxi-Fujian. On November 7, 1931 a Chinese Soviet Republic was declared, with Mao Zedong presiding over the Central Executive Committee and the Council of People's Commissariats, a true power next to the tatters of the "Shanghai Muscovites." In spite of the presence of a representative of the Central Committee, and that of Zhang Guotao (leader of the biggest base outside Jiangxi), Mao seemed in a position to take the reins of the Party.

The opposite occurred, however, in 1932. Mao was dispossessed of his base and "his" revolution by refugees from Shanghai; Zhou Enlai replaced him as Commissar of the Armies in 1933, and Zhang Wentian became head of the Soviet Republic in 1934. By pushing forward toward Shanghai after invading Manchuria (January 1932), Japan incited the Communists to enlarge the theater of operations. A new offensive on Wuhan, and Lin Biao's penetrating advance to Fujian, led Chiang Kai-shek to change his priorities. In the spring of 1932 he signed an agreement with the Japanese, and attacked Zhang Guotao's base north of the Yangtze, from which he could threaten Wuhan and Nanking. After having driven out Zhang, who began a Long March (three years before Mao's) in the direction of Sichuan, Chiang began a fourth campaign against Ruijin. Mao wanted to respond using guerrilla warfare, but Zhou Enlai and the Central Committee members saw a chance to widen the offensive strategy begun earlier that year. This quarrel symbolized two opposing conceptions and above all two opposing realities of the rural revolution and the army.

Mao's forces emerged decimated from the fighting of 1931. Mao's concern for quality prevented him from recruiting en masse. His enemies cared more for troops than for militants, and found his tactic evidence of hopeless Hunanese localism. They instituted a draft, and took in enemy deserters, aiming to drown the Maoists by sheer number. As for guerrilla activity, the best generals, behind Peng Dehuai, thought that the consolidation of the Soviets rendered it obsolete. Their plan was to fight a war of professionals, with the goal of denying Chiang's army access to the Communist strongholds.

"The bases are like the buttocks: without them an army cannot rest, and must run to exhaustion." What Mao called—contrary to Li Lisan—consolidating the bases and the army consisted in holding a territory, but the territory was not the ultimate goal. Institutionalized revolution was rearing its ugly head, and Mao's activism was threatened. In reality, his project for instituting rural reform, in which he had great hopes as a tool for permanent mobilization, became an annex of the draft. Like Prussia under Frederic II, Jiangxi was not a State with an Army (Prussia had 200,000, whereas Mao had only 50,000), but an Army with a State, which knew how to use against Mao the weapons—police intimidation, institutional obfus-cation, and political re-

Zhou Enlai, the aristocrat of the CCP, born in 1898 in the low Yangzi region, died in 1976 (like Mao and Zhu De), did not have (nor did Zhu) the calling to be the brilliant second-in-command that the legend and the reports of the Long March made him out to be (the period during which this photograph was taken). In 1933, he became the leader of the CPP, Wang Ming being in Moscow and Mao having been thrown into ineffectual opposition.
Ph © Roger Pic

education—he would himself adopt, having felt their efficiency firsthand. Indeed, the Central Committee of Fujian and its leaders (among them Deng Xiaoping, back from France via the Sun Yat-sen University in Moscow) had allowed the enemy to penetrate, whereas Chiang's fourth campaign had been repelled everywhere else. This served as a negative example in the context of a vast purge of the Party and the Army that was designed to sap Mao's influence.

Indeed, except for Lin Biao, the hierarchy turned a deaf ear to Mao. Although a constructive rebel, concerned with building a new order, Mao also represented a tendency Communist leaders considered archaic. Illustrating one of the deeper ambiguities of the Revolution with respect to the Empire, Mao completely denied the imperial dimension, earning himself the sobriquet of "frog at the bottom of the well" (Peng Dehuai) and the reputation of a "backward-looking and petite-bourgeoise peasant." The general sentiment was no longer toward a compromise with Chiang, but rather toward the foundation of a communist empire. Zhou Enlai claimed and obtained leadership of the Party because

he had steered it through the inevitable passage out of the Eden of rural, heroic communism, through the Fall into Statehood. This victory was as ephemeral as the circumstances that led to it, for Chiang's fifth campaign proved decisive, and Zhou's defeat left the way open for Mao.

The Wanderer

To be reborn, Mao had to wander. In late 1933, Japanese encroachments south of the Great Wall, and a rebellion of the Fujian Nationalists against Chiang's unchanged priorities, were delaying factors. The Communist Party leaders' talks with the rebels were compromised by Mao's draconian demands—not that he had any power over the negotiations, but the effect was sufficient to remove him from Ruijin, placing him under house arrest. Exclusion from the Party was the next logical step. Moreover, in May, he had ordered local commanders, Hunanese veterans, to use guerrilla tactics; Braun was enraged at this new insubordination. But his authority dwindled as fast as events unfolded. Mao remained steadfast and continued to rebel—first via Lin Biao in early July, then openly when defeat became imminent. The Party's immobility was catastrophic; even guerrilla warfare was useless at this point. The Jiangxi base had to be evacuated to save the army.

The Long March and the Conference of Zunyi mark the start of the last phase in Mao's rise to power. By bringing together Zhou Enlai, Liu Shaoqi (returned from Jiangxi in 1932), Chen Yun (another urban communist), and the generals, the March and the Conference would give military command over to Mao. This placed him at the center of Communist politics, but his position was vulnerable. Zhang Guotao, who had already achieved his Long March, carried considerable weight with military chiefs, who were impressed by the discipline of his well-equipped army. Only the providential defeat of his adversaries confirmed Mao's pre-eminence, which would not be questioned again

Starting in late 1933, Chiang's fifth campaign opposed his German advisers—shown here—against the German chief of the Komintern delegation, Otto Braun, alias Hua Fu (1901–1974). Braun was the last in a long line of Kremlin Proconsuls in China after Maring, Borodin, Lominadze, and Pavel Mif.
Ph © Roger-Viollet

until Wang Ming's attack in 1938. True, the Zunyi Conference did not eliminate all of his enemies, among whom "internationalists" such as Zhang Wentian, who had replaced Qin Bangxian (one of the main targets of the purge with Braun) within the Party Secretariat. In fact, Zunyi is one of the founding myths of Maoism, a reconstruction of the following decade, which heralded Mao's definitive rise to the top of a national Communist entity. From this entity, the "internationalists" would be sidelined by a coalition between Mao, Liu Shaoqi, Zhou Enlai, and the Army, which would dominate the Party until the Cultural Revolution.

Chiang Kai-shek deprived the Communists of their base, and forced them to run themselves to exhaustion. But the head of the movement was safe. Mao and ten thousand survivors set up camp in October 1935 at Bao'an, at the center of territory held by Gao Gang north of the Shaanxi. American journalists (Snow, Nym Wales, Agnes Smedley) discovered a troglodytic universe of caves, deep in the heart of "Yellow" China. And yet, resistance to the Japanese invaders allowed

THE LONG MARCH AND ITS LEGENDS

The Communists did not "march" at random; they headed toward the frontlines of the anti-Japanese resistance, based in the North and West of China. One hundred thousand men escaped Chiang's vigilance and headed southwest after a diversion to the northeast (see map). Avoiding compact columns, advancing by forced marches, many men were lost, died of sickness, or deserted. But they reached Guizhou Province, and a halt at Zunyi (January 1935) enabled Mao to draw the political conclusions of defeat. Geography itself was a bitter foe at the confines of Tibet, with snowbound passes and old chain bridges over tumultuous rivers. The Luding Bridge over the Dadu River was seized in the spring of 1935, allowing Mao to join Zhang Guotao's army further to the east. Dashing Chiang's hopes, the Communists succeeded in crossing terrain that had defeated Shi Dakai. Like Hannibal or Napoleon traversing the Alps, everything gave the episode superhuman proportions that Mao magnified in his poetry and his propaganda later on. Mao had to negotiate with Tibetan chieftains and fight Muslim troops guarding the great swamps of Gansu Province that barred the way to the north. (They would crush Zhang Guotao's army.) Zhang had broken with Mao; he contested the supremacy Mao gained as a result from his absence at the Zunyi Conference. Zhang might have forced Zhu De and other influential chiefs, but power vacillated once again. The Long Marches and their leaders' had taken their toll. Zhang's defeat as well as other lucky circumstances would allow Mao to achieve his goal, and begin erasing the luck behind the myth. ■

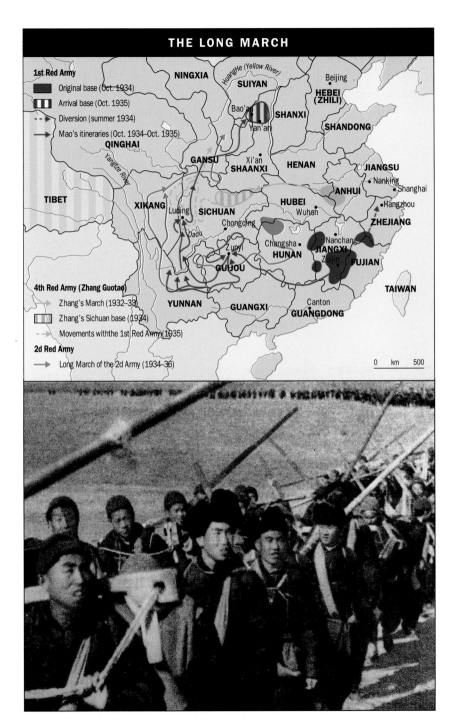

THE LONG MARCH

1st Red Army
- Original base (Oct. 1934)
- Arrival base (Oct. 1935)
- Diversion (summer 1934)
- Mao's itineraries (Oct. 1934–Oct. 1935)

4th Red Army (Zhang Guotao)
- Zhang's March (1932–35)
- Zhang's Sichuan base (1934)
- Movements with the 1st Red Army (1935)

2d Red Army
- Long March of the 2d Army (1934–36)

NINGXIA SUIYAN HuangHe (Yellow River) Beijing HEBEI (ZHILI) SHANXI Bao'an Yan'an SHANDONG QINGHAI GANSU Xi'an SHAANXI HENAN JIANGSU Nanking Shanghai Yangtze River Hangzhou TIBET XIKANG Luding SICHUAN Chongqing HUBEI Wuhan ZHEJIANG Dadu Zunyi Changsha Nanchang JIANGXI Ruijin FUJIAN GUIJOU HUNAN TAIWAN YUNNAN GUANGXI Canton GUANGDONG

0   km   500

the Communists to come out of isolation. Mao finally obtained the national arena that had been lacking at Jiangxi. The prospect of power in a reconstituted Empire was opening up to Mao, further justifying the Long March—which had been nothing but the last resort of a stubborn rebellion. It is no wonder that it became for Mao a boundless source of political, and poetical, inspiration. The poet is master of the world in Mao's cosmic vision, just as the politician takes power and makes China's history his own, through the sheer will to struggle and persevere.

> Now I tell you, Kunlun:
> Enough of your big airs, enough of this snow!
> If only I could, leaning against the sky, draw the
>   precious sword
> To cut you up into three parts!
> I would leave one to Europe,

I would give one to America,
And I would return one to the Eastern countries.
Then, a great peace would ensue in the world,
The terrestrial globe would bring together your wintry
        weather and your blazing heat.

(Kunlun, October 1935)

When the Long March ended, the Communists set up camp at Bao'an, north of the Shanxi. Yanan was occupied a year later, in late 1936. The caves that the Communists inhabited until the spring of 1947 became part of the legend of the Long March. With its checkerboard administrative center, the cradle of Maoism symbolizes the imperial vision that became Mao's after the Japanese invasion.
Ph © Roger Pic

Chapter 5

EMPIRE **A**SSUMED

19**36**–19**54**

ESTABLISHED AT YANAN AT THE END OF THE LONG MARCH,
MAO IMPLEMENTED HIS ACTIVIST PRECEPTS BY ORGANIZING THE
POPULATION AND FORGING A PARTY-STATE THAT WOULD ENABLE
HIM TO EMBARK UPON THE POLITICAL AND MILITARY CONQUEST
OF CHINA.

Mao Zedong tamed the rebel within by satisfying its demands rather than repressing them. When he assumed power, it was on a scale that was acceptable to him: over the State, over the Army, but also over guerrilla strategy and mass activism. His maturity and success depended on this compromise between Mao the Rebel and Mao the Emperor, that was to be almost twenty years in the making (1936–1954, from rebuilding the Party at Yanan to the first quarrels about the destiny of socialist China). Mao's imperial vision, revived on a foundation of anti-Japanese resistance, would extend throughout China, from the territory (1949) to the people (1954).

The principles established at Yanan triumphed thanks to the acceleration of events, including the Korean War (1950–53). As in 1895, Japanese aggression gave Maoism a powerful impetus. The opportunity still had to be successfully exploited; nothing was granted at the outset. But Mao was a consummate political and military chief. Two decades of experience had strengthened his judgment—without, of course, making him infallible, as his personality cult would later suggest. Another test was to come in 1936–38, with the Xi'an crisis and the threat of a new rival: Wang Ming.

Soldiers of the Red Army (re-dubbed the 8th Army of the Road) at Yanan. Just as it was Lenin's best ally in 1917, war—against Japan, against the Guomindang, then against the US in Korea—was instrumental in Mao's passage from rebellion to the conquest of power within the Party (1945), the nation (1949), and Chinese society as a whole (1954).
Ph © Roger Pic

Resistance, the Cradle of Maoism

After his triumph over Wang Ming (see sidebar), Mao imposed a strategy dependent neither on the cities nor on Moscow. The Japanese invasion, by shattering Blue China's political movements, and by separating on the ground the two parts of the Front, left Mao's rural guerrilla warfare as the only valid option. Providing this vision of an independent communist strategy, Mao rallied nationalist elements within the Party who had stood by him at Zunyi against Braun. Liu Shaoqi, an urban Communist, was his staunchest supporter against Wang Ming, in the

Japanese troops enter the Forbidden City in occupied Beijing (July 1937). The war neutralized Chiang Kai-shek's anti-communist crusade; it also annihilated efforts to modernize undertaken by the Nanking government, and facilitated the strategy of surrounding cities from the countryside.
Ph © Coll. Viollet

interests of Party autonomy. In concert with Mao, he would undertake the "Maoization" of the Party, breaking with its internationalist legacy. But this remained an internal matter. Soviet Communism was still a source of ideological and institutional inspiration. Actual conflict with Moscow would be twenty more years in the making.

While the war had paralyzed Chiang Kai-shek, nationalism facilitated the birth of the Red State. Maoist doctrine has emphasized the "revolutionary" aspect of this transformation, invoking the massive support of an impoverished peasantry convinced in the truth of communism's liberating message. Peasant mobilization was the key to communism's rise, but it was achieved with a political framework.

Part of this was the strategy of union that Mao formulated in 1940 in "New Democracy." Following his analyses of the twenties, Mao explained that war-torn China was at an historic juncture in terms of the unity of classes. Workers, peasants, and intellectuals were joined by elements of the bourgeoisie whose nationalism made them "anti-bureaucratic" (in other words,

XI'AN AND WANG MING'S CHALLENGE

December 1936: as Chiang was being captured by commanders of the anti-communist blockade hostile to his policies, maneuvers started in view of creating a second United Front (1937–1945). The Generalissimo (Chiang) was forced to accept national unity, and Mao had to accept the Generalissimo. Mao's 1935 principle of "Union at the Base" excluded a priori Chiang, but Stalin held to his analysis of the twenties: national unity depended on Chiang's participation, all the more because of the international fascist threat. Wang Ming said as much at the Fifth Komintern Congress at which the strategy of union was revived, and from there all that was necessary was to have their enemy freed. The Communists, invited to the talks at Xi'an, sent Zhou Enlai as their emissary. Since the telephone line had been reopened with Moscow, the Communists could no longer turn a deaf ear to the Kremlin's injunctions. The Japanese invasion (July 1937) nullified the agreement signed

two months later. The Communists recognized the supremacy of the central government, and their armies (the Northern Army became the 8th Army of the Road) were in theory to be integrated with Chiang's forces, while keeping their separate territories and internal organization. In Wang Ming's nostalgic view of a "Blue" communist China, the alliance with Chiang was to allow a new focus on the cities. Liu Shaoqi had revitalized the CCP's influence over the new anti-Chiang student movements. Negotiations with the Guomindang seemed to open up the possibility of renewed militant activity. At Yanan, Mao's intransigence was not unanimously echoed when Wang Ming made a visit there (December 1937) to impose his vision of the Second Front. Mao put on a warm show for the Kremlin envoy, to stir up solidarity and national feeling among his companions, but he was no longer the local official, the Party subordinate of five years before. In fact, the crisis was unfolding not far from Yanan, in Wuhan where Chiang's

government had retreated. With the Japanese occupying the city, the right and left wings of the Front fought over control, just as in 1927. The authorities outlawed mass organizations mobilized by the CCP to defend the city. Wang Ming arrived to negotiate, and rejected the order to evacuate sent by the Yanan Central Committee, once again in Mao's hands after Ming's departure. The fall of Wuhan in October sealed the fate of Wang's attempt, which was condemned by the Sixth Central Committee Plenum (Oct.–Nov. 1938). Once again, Mao Zedong had achieved victory through his rival's opportune defeat—a victory as important as the Zunyi Conference of 1935. The Second United Front survived until 1945, mainly thanks to the physical separation of the partner-enemies caused by the war, but also thanks to Mao's determination to maintain an isolated Communist State. ∎

against the pro-Japanese regime), and wealthy landowners in the villages controlled by the Communists, who were only too eager to cooperate in areas threatened by Japanese invasion. In these areas the CCP formally shared power with the Guomindang as well as a few third parties, and elections were organized. This open-mindedness won the Communists the support of a good number of urban intellectuals, artists, and writers who preferred to go to Yanan rather than to Guomindang-controlled areas to escape the Japanese occupation of the cities.

Mao involved the rural elite in politics through his strategy of union, but they were already prominent within the rural power structure. The only concession the CCP made to the Second Front was to halt land expropriation, and to apply the agrarian reform planned by the defunct Nanking government (a cap on rents, moderate taxation). It was by cleverly exploiting nationalistic fervor that peasant mobilization succeeded, increasing CCP influence on a national level. Mao crystallized peasant nationalism by awakening and politicizing a traditional xenophobia, dormant since the Boxer Rebellion.

The Communists' skill in organizing local resistance made them both the artisans and the chief beneficiaries of this effort. To be sure, their presence also led to terror raids on the villages by the Japanese Army. In this way, the revolutionary movement changed in quality as well as scale. Like Tito in Yugoslavia, Mao presided over a new socialism whose "path" would lead to a definitive break with the Soviet Union.

Thanks to Mao's clever use of nationalistic sentiment, of the dichotomy between the Communists and the Guomindang, and of his own activist skills, the peasantry was mobilized in a new and powerful way. Mao aimed this weapon at will according to place and circumstance: on the occupant, of course, or the pro-Japanese authorities in the disputed regions. In Communist-controlled territory, the targets were landlords resistant to agrarian reform or peasants who balked at orders to produce more.

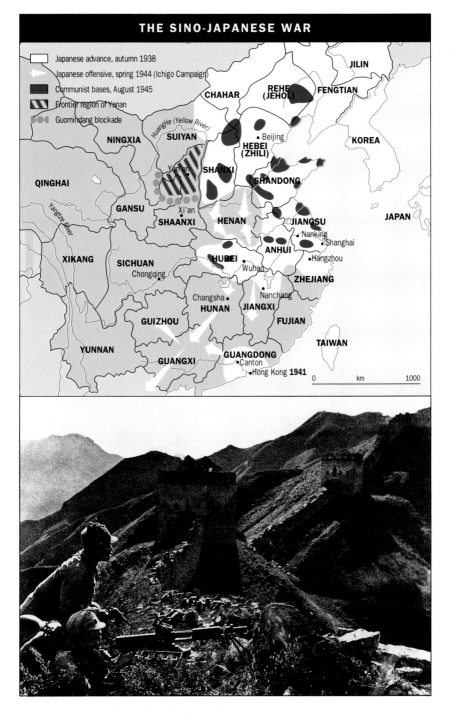

THE SINO-JAPANESE WAR

Japanese advance, autumn 1938

Japanese offensive, spring 1944 (Ichigo Campaign)

Communist bases, August 1945

Frontier region of Yenan

Guomindang blockade

JILIN

FENGTIAN

CHAHAR

REHE (JEHOL)

KOREA

SUIYAN

HuangHe (Yellow River)

NINGXIA

Beijing

HEBEI (ZHILI)

SHANXI

Yán'an

SHANDONG

QINGHAI

GANSU

Xi'an

JAPAN

SHAANXI

HENAN

JIANGSU

Yangtze River

Nanking

Shanghai

XIKANG

ANHUI

Hangzhou

SICHUAN

HUBEI

Chongqing

Wuhan

ZHEJIANG

Changsha

Nanchang

HUNAN

JIANGXI

FUJIAN

GUIZHOU

TAIWAN

YUNNAN

GUANGDONG

Canton

GUANGXI

Hong Kong 1941

0   km   1000

Yanan, 1942. Concerted mobilization of the masses in the context of wartime productivity was one of the main levers by which the Party, under cover of unity and democracy, was able to install structures of control. These would form the foundation of the future totalitarian Maoist state.
Ph © Wu Yinxian/Magnum

As in Jiangxi, the Communists' power was consolidated at the level of village "micropolitics," whose scope was widened in the context of anti-Japanese resistance. The enemy polarized the masses to such a degree that the Communists were able to utilize the existing power structures instead of doing away with them. When the Communists were forced to evacuate a territory or occupy it only partially, the peasants were less inclined to hold it against them. Of course, the CCP was not an ally like any other; it dominated the society that it mobilized. Nationalistic sentiment saved Maoism from having to liquidate its class enemies and allowed it to devote all its energy to solidifying its hegemony over the masses. Mao spared no pains, and took all the time necessary to implant his ideas and his methods in the rural base. There was a world of difference between the guerrillas supported by the Guomindang, Communists' own ruinous ventures of the twenties, and Soviet Communism, which had a marked preference for the urban proletariat.

The Tools of Maoism

The legacy of Jiangxi—a politicized army, propaganda campaigns based on the "mass line," and the pitiless re-education of militants—was enhanced at Yanan, developed and institutionalized. Domination and the re-education of intellectuals was indeed a crucial step.

Many have tried to understand Maoism as the incarnation of democracy in its purest state, almost an antidote to Stalinist totalitarianism. The Yananese miracle did embody new contact between a backward rural society and a political elite professing an egalitarian ideology—a contact that took place far from urban comforts. Of course, Yananese society was already diverse, and the arrival of urban intellectuals and politicians further widened the gap between the elite and the peasants. The Guomindang had also considerably shaken up the social landscape when it installed itself en masse in Sichuan and Yunan Provinces.

The intellectuals' mission was no longer to guide the people, but to catalyze the mobilization process by creating positive narratives: heroic figures peopled Maoist morality plays, in which the "line" was disseminated in dramatic and entertaining form. Here, a musical given at Yanan in 1943. Ph © Wu Yinxian/Magnum

We must gather the

ideas of the masses,

analyze them,

concentrate them into

general and systematic

ideas, then return

before the masses to

spread and explain

them, in such a way

Mao's ambition was to forge total unity, and he imposed his activist mentality by homogenizing differences. Rural China had to catch up, and it had to defeat the enemy: the sacred union justified all forms of integration. The concept of the struggle was Maoist activism's binding glue; it cemented together a mass of contradictions in a state of perpetual development.

Mao was finally in a position to elaborate a political discourse shared by the authorities and the people— an ideal that dated from the time of the anti-Manchu revolutionaries and the May 4th activists. Maoist thought integrated a vision of society as a permanent conflict of people and ideas that he had developed in the twenties and thirties. This was no longer the rhetoric of popular culture, rebel religion, or intellectual tradition, but a new idiom, entirely the work of Communist leaders, which drew on a multitude of references, Communist and non-communist, Chinese or foreign, to create the fundamentals of the Revolution. With the key instruments of the right line and re-education, Maoism tapped at will into the vast energies of "Yellow" China. The challenge of winning

THE ABC'S OF MAOISM:

In the villages held by Communist forces, the peasants were assembled to debate on Party platforms. Resistance against the Japanese, elections, army and militia recruitment, application of agrarian laws, organization of cooperatives in view of improving agricultural productivity, literacy campaigns, the emancipation of women—these issues did not come up by chance, nor through the spontaneity of the masses, which were intensely acted upon by professional agitators. Communist militants sang the praise of local heroes and heroines,

whether they were soldiers, workers, or peasants. They also vituperated against "counter-exemplary" elements of society—bad landlords, collaborators, even bad Communists— without ever putting into question Party authority. In the case of criticism within the Party, blame was laid on "faulty methods"; "formalist," "bureaucratic," or "feudal" were other adjectives used to describe corruption or incompetence. "Rectification" was an organized process, from preliminary hearings to final judgment and sentencing (usually reeducation or suspension). Higher-level

officials supervised these internal dramas and dictated their outcome. They thus had total oversight over the application of the Party line, while inviting the masses to criticize it. But the Party always kept the initiative, which to Mao was essential in a fluid situation. It made a few strategic concessions (for example, attenuating reforms on marriage to which most clan chiefs were hostile), and imposed its will the rest of the time: forcing a new kind of solidarity and cooperative labor that went against many peasant traditions. The Communist leader knew that total victory was a mirage, and over the countryside had been successful. While the old Yellow mainstays—peasantry and bureaucracy—were now those of the Communist Party, their positive attributes (austerity, simplicity, the affected camaraderie of egalitarianism) helped mask what was more difficult to accept.

The new political style, which would define the People's Republic, created an intense climate of struggle, of permanent education, and of mental and physical mobilization. People were encouraged to perfect themselves in work and stay clear of "bookish" dogmatism. The foundations of this edifice of theory and practice were laid in 1936–37: the lessons of guerrilla warfare in "Strategic Problems of Revolutionary War" (1936), and the key concepts of "practice" and "contradiction" in his conferences of July and August 1937. The Party and the Army being both the reflection and the vital nerve of the whole, the Revolution necessitated building both with great care. Recruitment of militants was stepped up, and specialized training schools were opened for those destined to climb the party ladder. This meticulous

that they adhere to them and put them into action, and finally, verify the rightness of these ideas through their translation into the actions of the masses.

Mao Zedong, June 1943

THE RIGHT LINE AND RECTIFICATION

that what counted was to retain control over the process of politicization in which society as a whole—including the sphere of power—was involved. This was not to be achieved by "pluralizing" public opinion or through recourse to counter-authorities, but by obtaining the participation of a homogenized whole in a political struggle led by the Communist elite. Self-criticism and education by initiation to peasant life were a way to present Communist leaders as examples of the "right line"—the strict discipline and combative spirit acquired during the Long March—while attributing these qualities to

the masses. This allowed Mao Zedong to present his "right ideas" as originating with the people… Intellectuals, writers, and artists played a special role. No longer the natural leaders of the people, their mission was to educate the people and re-educate themselves. This meant training one ear on the people, the better to tailor their creations to popular taste, and another on orders from above to produce works that directly addressed issues such as the work ethic, failure to re-educate, or self-criticism—never putting into question the nature of power or the personalities who wielded it

within the Party. On occasion, and increasingly after the great rectification movement of 1942 (when Mao established the rules of the game in his speeches at the Forum of Art and Literature), intellectuals guilty of "mixing genres" became useful negative examples. Most were reintegrated after self-criticism; attacking "deviant" intellectuals was soon a regular ingredient in propaganda campaigns. One of them, who refused the role of apostate, was thrown in prison (for Trotskyism) and executed during the evacuation of Yanan in 1947. ∎

organization, coupled with the attention to political indoctrination and verification of conduct, produced a genuine miracle of an Army that was accepted by the people. Standards and rituals were inculcated through the practices of discussion groups that assembled to explain the Party line, to evaluate people's individual conduct, and to mediate criticism and self-criticism. Party leaders codified it all in published manuals such as *How to Become a Good Member of the Communist Party* (Liu Shaoqi, first printing in July 1939), which became the most-printed book in China, until it was supplanted by Mao's own Little Red Book during the Cultural Revolution.

From 1942 to 1944, the essential communist literature, by Mao and others, was compiled in an anthology of extracts that was meant to be the bible of the "Movement for the Rectification of the Work Ethic" (*Zhengfeng*), the most important and decisive operation of the Yananese period. The leaders cemented their control over the rapidly expanding party and the small community of intellectuals: homogenization was becoming Maoization. The last traces of the Party's "internationalist" past had been eradicated, definitively associated by Liu Shaoqi with

the infamous epithet of "Menshevik" in July 1943.
The General Secretariat, headed by Zhang Wentian,
an internationalist who had rallied Mao's camp in
Zun'yi, fell into oblivion. Mao's ascension within the
Party was nearly complete. Henceforth, every area of
Chinese thought, from philosophy to history, would
bear the indelible stamp of Mao's thought, as
collectively expressed and formulated by a team of
loyal lieutenants. Not only Mao's thought, but also
his person, became a manufactured legend. The
1945 "Resolution," in which Mao consigned this
myth in a narrative saga relating the struggle of his
"right line" against "deviation," came out shortly
before the Seventh Congress of the Chinese
Communist Party. At the end of this gathering of
leaders and delegates, the *Zhengfeng* had acquired
canonic status (alongside Marx and Lenin), and Mao
had been named President of the Central Committee.

*The Maoist strategy of encircling
the cities from the countryside
necessitated unceasing growth
on the part of the army.
Militants and militias training
here in Yanan in 1939 were far
from the romance of early 20th-
century rebellions
Ph © Walter Bosshard/Magnum*

The Contradictions of President Mao

Subtle and impossible to classify, Mao's theories
integrate his personal hesitations and ambiguities. His
dual nature—rebel, despot—and political vision—
revolutionary, imperial—projected themselves and

The law of

contradiction inherent

in things and in

phenomena, or the law

of identical opposites, is

the fundamental law

of dialectical

materialism...

Mao Zedong, August 1937

their demands on Yananese society. There was abuse, privilege, and repression; there was also much dynamism. Mao's selective borrowing from Stalin should be seen in this light. The contradiction between a State and Party apparatus and the Revolution was judged "secondary." Although Mao would change his mind once he had to regain power, the apparatus was accepted and recognized as a necessary evil, to be combated in a non-antagonistic manner—avoiding "dogmatism" and "bureaucratism." The result was the implantation of a Stalinist apparatus throughout the Yanan region, a ponderous and pitiless regime.

The Chinese gulag, or "forgotten archipelago" in the words of French historian Jean-Luc Domenach, where political enemies were relegated, was already a real phenomenon in Yanan. The *laogai* ("reform through work") were thinly disguised labor camps, whose existence bore witness to the accelerating evolution toward a police state. The regime's bureaucratic tendency asserted itself openly at Yanan. Prominent figures were now officers, political educators, policemen, and Party officials, replacing intellectuals, union officials, and guerrillas at the top of the social and political hierarchy. This had been intended by the Communists, who sought literally to remold society. Its stratifications and mechanisms, rituals, uses and abuses of power, all bore the stamp of the Maoist way—including a few novel customs, such as abandoning militant wives for intellectuals or artists from the coastal areas.

While Stalinist influences were important in forging Maoism's unique blend of rigidity and activism, the core Marxist ideas were vastly modified from the original. His works, as well as those of Lenin, had been made available in Chinese translation since the twenties. But the excerpts that were to be the subject of debate at Yanan were the biased commentaries of Stalinist Russia, which often distorted the original ideas. Mao's writings reflected this, in their tendency to emphasize "normalized" Marxist discourse; they also relied heavily on contributions of Chinese specialists who would become the future cadres of the Institutes of the People's Republic, temples of onferences in August 1937 contextualized the contradictory essence of politics within the fundamental contradictions of the human and natural universe: contra-diction was everywhere, a cosmic and social principle. Knowledge and theory were considered forms of action and struggle; the contradiction between them is at the heart of dialectical materialism. Phases of struggle and phases of unity alternate, according to the inevitably gradual nature of human progress. The Party's mission was to manage this process, in the wisdom of its guiding line. It also fashioned the political, moral and social distinctions of the political and social arena: poor, middling or rich peasants, good or bad landowners, good or bad Party officials. Finally, it decreed which categories were allies or enemies, and which contradictions were internal (concerning the people) or external and therefore "antagonistic." On the one hand, the contradictions from within could be resolved (faulty work ethic, enduring feudalism among landowners tolerated by the New Democracy, etc.). These were "secondary" and "non-antagonistic." By strict re-education, by ritualizing and controlling political conflict, the Party was confident in its ability to exploit it to its own advantage. But in its "primary" or "antagonistic" aspect, contradiction threatened the very source of political authority. Personified successively by Japan, the Guomindang, feudal landlords, the enemy was finally designated as the bourgeoisie—as in "bourgeois" tendencies in the Party, to be eradicated at all costs. In truth, despite the democratic energy of dialectical materialsim, the Party's firm "guiding line" and re-education programs forced critics of Communism and the Party either to re-educate themselves, or face elimination. In this way the political process contributed to the Communists' goal: the creation of a homogeneous society. Activism was now fully geared to the extension of Communist power and its perpetuation, "dialectically"—or not! ∎

Ph © Roger Pic

*J*iang Qing (1914–1991). After the scorned peasant girl, the martyred intellectual (Yang Kaihui), and the long-suffering militant (He Zizhen, exhausted companion of the Long March, evacuated to Moscow in 1937), the actress from Shanghai would remain with Mao from 1938 to his death.
Ph © Archives CDCC

Chinese Marxism-Leninism.

The most prominent purveyor of orthodox Marxism —which Mao had little taste for—was none other than his secretary, Chen Boda. This throwback to the Chinese Communist romantic, poetical roots rekindled the fires of dialectical materialism by injecting the concept of primacy of the will, of ideas tested through action. The "subjective" was to conquer the "objective" within the unfolding of historical contradiction. One must not exaggerate the philosophical rigor of this discourse, as some Western intellectuals did in the 1960s and 1970s. The true strength of Maoist thinking lies in its complete attunement to a precise time and a political situation, and centered upon a personality who was mainly a technician and a tactician who despised bureaucrats and intellectuals—modern incarnations of the mandarins Mao had hated since childhood. Adopting an affected humility, Mao was the master in student's garb, a dictator in the making with a provocateur's tongue and an iconoclast's wit. It was this subtle but explosive cocktail that enabled him to disrupt and reconstruct a social hierarchy over which he had total control.

More than his Spartan attire or his down-to-earth manner with the people (diligently imitated by Party officials and oligarchs), his speeches best illustrate the complex underpinnings of his mind. Vituperating ritual, including Communist ones ("dogmatism" in his view), the hardened pedagogue did not hesitate to pepper his denunciations with foul language, a distinctly scatological tendency that Western intellectuals promptly analyzed from a Freudian point of view. Indeed, Mao's double nature—rebel/ruler, iconoclast/founder of an orthodoxy—went beyond his words and deeds. It was reflected and embodied in the two kinds of Maoisms that coexisted in Yanan.

The Yanan Coalition

In contrast with the eccentric, even cavalier, personal style of Mao, who enjoyed nothing more than disturbing the established order of things to assert his own power, Liu Shaoqi and Chen Yun (another urban

Communist leader who had joined Mao at Zun'yi, just like Liu) represented a more staid vision, more preoccupied with authority, institutions, and hierarchies. Once institutional power had taken the place of revolutionary action and "socialist" China had been ridden of its class enemies, these different sensibilities would clash. For the moment, at Yanan, the fight against the Japanese and their Chinese collaborators completely monopolized the people's hostility. Mao played the role of captain of a team who supported him, even magnifying his aura of prestige against Chiang Kai-shek, who had made a comeback: Mao's personality cult was underway.

Like the political institutions created during the war, the style of leadership forged in the 1940s would remain the pivot of the People's Republic until the Cultural Revolution. Mao refused the concept of collegiality— but neither was he a despot or a tyrant. Power at the summit was not yet in the hands of a clan chief engaged in factional strife, but shared among a group of men who knew each other personally, whose ideologies were sometimes divergent and who belonged to different strata of the Party society. The Party and the Army had their own agendas. The historian Roderick MacFarqhuar invoked Camelot and the Round Table; one might also be reminded of *Water Margin*. Peng Duhuai gradually took over from Zhu De in the role of "commander." Zhou Enlai, in spite of being in distant Chungking (as representative to Chiang Kai-shek), remained in the top three at least until 1945, as negotiator and later as Prime

This portrait of Mao and Jiang Qing was signed and dedicated to Stalin's representative in Yanan. She agreed to remain in the shadows, for her tempestuous past risked tarnishing Mao's image. Twenty years later, she would burst into the limelight, as high priestess of the Cultural Revolution. She was condemned to death in 1981 (commuted later) and committed suicide in 1991, never renouncing her extremist views.
Ph © Archives CDCC

*"**W**e must [...] say [to those who have a dogmatic practice of communism]: 'Your dogma serves no purpose.' To put it less politely, 'Your dogma is less useful than excrement. Even dog manure can be used as fertilizer. A dog can eat human excrement. Dogma can neither fertilize a field nor nourish a canine. It is utterly useless." In a speech inaugurating the Zhengfeng in February 1942, the iconoclastic rebel founded a new ritual of authority in his denunciation of rituals.*
Ph © Archives CDCC

Minister. In second place, Mao Zedong's alter ego, Liu Shaoqi, ran the Party. Chen Yun (fifth in the hierarchy) was the economic brains of the team, and the only former worker.

After the tumult of the Cultural Revolution, this ecumenical form of Maoism would again become the norm. The 1940s left an indelible imprint on political customs that would outlast its protagonists' political entente. Deng Xiaoping exploited this legacy with great skill, as a symbol of Chinese identity and values, although in a manner once again geared to authoritarian rather than activist political control. After de-Maoization, the memory of Liu, Zhou, and Zhu was associated with that of Mao at the Tiananmen Mausoleum: the Party, the Army, and the State united around a chief who reigned as a charismatic federator of China, and creator of consensus within the Communist Party.

The coalition of Yanan owed its success—but also its fragility—to the fact that Mao and Maoism reached a point of delicate equilibrium in the mid-1940s, much more because of external circumstances than Mao's own political maturity. At any rate there ensued a

decade (1945–54) during which the Yananese machine was able to re-conquer the Empire, and reorganize it in its image— until the time came when the emperor would become a rebel again, to force those around him to accede to his demands for building a socialist society. This was doubtless the only non-contradictory aspect of Mao's character: while he represented ambiguity at the reins of power, his exercise of power was in no way ambiguous.

*L*iu Shaoqi (at left), Mao's alter ego at Yanan, was an indispensable ally until the 1960s. Deng Xiaoping (at right), a secondary figure in the 1940s, kept his principles alive: the tutelary nature of power, ritual purges in the Party, and re-education of intellectuals, even within a period of de-Maoization and economic reform.
Ph © Wu Yinxian/Magnum

Military Conquest

During the few months preceding the final confrontation between the CCP and the Guomindang (summer 1945–spring 1946), politicians maneuvered for the first time in thirty years without war. The order of the day was coalition government, according to the formula Roosevelt pushed through at Yalta—with what he thought was Stalin's blessing. Mao did meet with Chiang Kai-shek at Chungking with the approval of Stalin, who had little expectation of the CCP winning the race to power. At the end of 1945, General Marshall, President Truman's envoy, brought together delegates from the Guomindang, the CCP, and a host of other third parties, as weak as they were divided among themselves.

In 1946, the situation between the countries now known as superpowers became more tense. Stalin was advancing his pawns, while Truman resisted. In China, conflict arose around Manchuria (occupied by the Soviets after they had declared war in extremis against Japan) in a manner that strongly foreshadowed the Cold War. Violence broke out there in the spring of 1946; the Communists withdrew from negotiations and launched an agrarian revolution, breaking symbolically with the Front.

The Guomindang benefited from American material

Let us unite, and make a clear distinction between ourselves and our enemies.

Mao Zedong, August 1952

and logistical aid; the CCP returned to guerrilla tactics. Until the summer of 1947, its forces were in retreat. Thirteen years after Ruijin, Yanan fell. Simultaneously, Communist leaders implemented a plan to use the agrarian revolution to reinforce the People's Liberation Army (PLA). The Party regained direct control over many villages during operations aimed at deposing big landowners. The techniques of political mobilization and control perfected at Yanan ensured the Party's hold on peasant society, from which it extracted huge numbers of soldiers and militants. The Guomindang reacted differently: Chiang Kai-shek spread out his divisions and extended communications, personally overseeing the conduct of operations. Wary of his generals, Chiang distrusted the provincial governors and the factions of his divided and corrupt regime. His movement lacked the cohesion and ideological dynamism of the Communists. And yet, although public opinion—especially students—opposed the war and American intervention, in 1946 the cities were still not about to throw themselves into the arms of the CCP. It

THE AGRARIAN REFORM (1946–1950)

Have you overthrown the corps today?" "Yes, but it was empty!" William Hinton's report on the agrarian reform in China (1946–50), "Fanshen," is an irreplaceable document. The "corps" is both the village elite, decimated by the Communist assault against the landowners, and the possessions of the "overthrown" class: land, villas, gold and silver money, and jewels. The peasants were able to assuage their thirst for vengeance during huge "struggle meetings" organized in each village; they would cost the lives of over five million landowners. But the spoils were disappointing. The roughly 40 percent of the land that was redistributed did not suffice to better the

situation of millions of paupers, even though each household had its own tiny piece of land. Moreover, the Communists had to defend the medium-sized farms, belonging to the peasant middle class, from the peasants. The 1947 feverish leveling of rural society was back to a semblance of Maoist normalcy a year later. In the process, the excesses of the first stage of the reform were halted, with all the usual public criticism of "leftist corruption" for good measure; this appeased the peasant masses, already groaning under the yoke of "work teams." This was the most important result of the agrarian reform, and it was a political one: the terrain was now prepared for

collectivization. By eliminating the intermediaries (the rural elite), the Party now had the peasants under direct control, and began to create its own rural elite. The rural nomenklatura, who owed everything to Mao, would be a key political lever for the Communist leader against the Party apparatus and the high-level apparatchiks throughout the 1950s. ∎

*P*easant accuses landlord during the agrarian reform.
Ph © Marc Riboud/Magnum

From August to October 1945, Mao negotiated with Chiang Kai-shek at Chungking. The Guomindang's resistance efforts and American support had made the Generalissimo an incontrovertible partner. The Communists played the game of coalition-building—presented as the New Democracy, which improved their standing in the cities.
Ph © Rapho

would take the delaying of democracy and agrarian reform for urban society to embrace Maoism.

The Nationalist government left the countryside to the notables, with whom it had forged an implicit alliance, only appearing to collect taxes, and recruit for the army and road work. While these activities did not create unrest in the areas where the Communists had no influence, they contributed to the degradation of the rural situation. Under nourished and poorly treated, the peasant-soldiers deserted at the first opportunity, and joined the Communists, who fed them, educated them, and politicized them—then gave them back their guns. By 1948, the Nationalist army was disintegrating, all to the benefit of the PLA.

In the same year, runaway inflation hit the cities, which fell out of Guomindang influence. Belated efforts at monetary conversion only increased speculation and aggravated the climate of mistrust. Whole regions capitulated and joined the Communists while the PLA was winning decisive victories, first in Manchuria, then against Chiang's last defensive bastion along the Huai River basin, between the Yellow and Yangtze Rivers (November–December 1948). While Mao was proclaiming the People's

Republic in Beijing on October 1st, his Army was marching south and west. After occupying Tibet in October 1950, only the Taiwanese Strait would stop the PLA's inexorable advance.

Political Conquest

Once the Chinese territory was secure within its former imperial boundaries, Mao could set about conquering the people in earnest. Agrarian and marital reform implemented in the wake of the PLA's advance in the south, consolidated the Party's hold on the villages. The countryside was in no way abandoned to improvised democracy, any more than it was to free markets. Party officials gradually took over the roles of the landlords and the merchants, the husbands and mothers-in-law. In the cities, the strict anti-inflationist policies of Chen Yun, and the strong public sector left by the Guomindang, enabled the Communists to control currency, the banks, and a significant portion of industry. The fledgling private sector of "national capitalism"—brainchild of the "New Democracy"—was kept at bay in every business by the unions and Party cells, busy whipping up recruits to reinforce the Party's proletarian base. Intellectuals were subjected to intense training sessions on Maoism and

By 1948, inflation and speculation had led to panic on a massive scale. The workers were protected to a degree by the sliding scale they had obtained, but civil servants, teachers, merchants, and businessmen were hit head on.
Ph © Henri Cartier-Bresson/Magnum

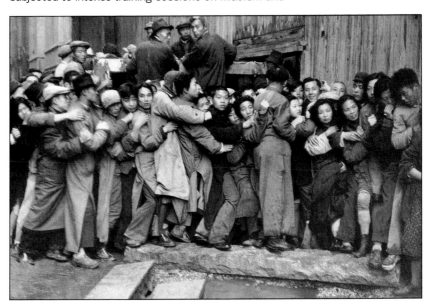

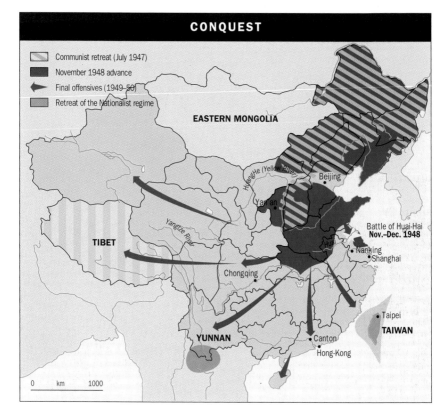

CONQUEST

- Communist retreat (July 1947)
- November 1948 advance
- Final offensives (1949–50)
- Retreat of the Nationalist regime

EASTERN MONGOLIA

Huang He (Yellow River)

Beijing

Yan'an

Battle of Huai-Hai
Nov.–Dec. 1948

Yangtze River

TIBET

Huai

Nanking
Shanghai

Chongqing

Taipei

TAIWAN

YUNNAN

Canton

Hong-Kong

0   km   1000

After crossing the Yangtze, the PLA advanced quickly to the Strait of Formosa, which protected the Nationalist government and three million refugees. The war against the "red bandits" waged by the Guomindang from Taiwan was not declared over until 1992.

the most "activist" ways to adopt its principles and practice them.

This "reform of thought", in which some Westerners saw certain human and pedagogical virtues, was in reality pure brainwashing, achieved through intimidation and fear. No one wanted to end up a victim of Party terror, which pitilessly eliminated enemies of the Party, or of society—gangsters, prostitutes, beggars—that it deemed no longer fit for re-education, or "irrecoverable" in the Leninist jargon. The specter of the *laogai* gave great weight to ideological campaigns, and one consequence was the creeping paralysis of the multitude of connections that crisscrossed Chinese society. Classmates, colleagues, and friends saw their relationships dissolve; the idiom of "socialist camaraderie" spread throughout a China penetrated at every level by representatives of mass organizations that relayed the messages and the edicts of the Party.

In contrast to the Guomindang of the thirties, which frittered away the spoils of victory, the Communists swallowed theirs whole, with a hearty totalitarian appetite. And obstacles served only to redouble their thirst for mobilization. Peasants were reluctant to

divorce, to cooperate, to pay taxes; intellectuals bucked at re-education, unions rose up against the Party bosses, the black market infiltrated contracts between the State and the private sector; fraud and corruption were rampant. In the countryside, agrarian reform was subverted by rookie officials, who defended the localities they headed against the Party apparatus. Resistance and failure only intensified Party ardor, further spurred on by the outbreak of war in Korea—a result of the Cold War and the treaty Mao had signed with Stalin in 1950. While the Chinese forces commanded by Peng Dehuai remained bogged down until the armistice of 1953, the internal front was progressing in leaps and bounds. The urban party apparatus was re-educated in 1951. At the end of the same year, the campaign extended to "national capitalists," who were hit with stiff fines and subjected to stronger political control, laying the ground for a wave of nationalizations in 1955–56.

The Communist debacle precipitated a defeat that Mao Zedong had foreseen since 1948, when he proclaimed a "return to the cities". The two Chinas were once again in contact, sharing the twentieth-century. Here, in Nanking, the peasant-soldiers of "Yellow" China marching into the heart of "Blue" China, were looked upon "as if they were Martians," in the words of Robert Guillain, who reported on the events in Shanghai.
Ph © Henri Cartier-Bresson/Magnum

Meanwhile, the first Five-Year Plan, based on the Soviet model, was implemented. The transition to socialism underway in the cities led to a closer link to the rural areas. In 1953, a system of requisitions replaced the commercial distribution circuits, enabling the State to convert profits from moving goods and agricultural products into capital that could be channeled into developing industry. The Party apparatus in the southern provinces was normalized through the arrival of thousands of Northerners. In order to exert optimum surveillance of a highly mobile population, the authorities multiplied control mechanisms. Pending all-out collectivization, peasants were enrolled in "labor units" (*danwei*), which distributed wages and bonuses, furnished housing, education and medical care, and organized leisure activities. City-dwellers' names were taken down in each neighborhood's Party Committee. Officials kept a close eye on the professional and private activities of everyone: teachers, students, workers, and civil servants all had their own file, kept rigorously up-to-date. Finally, individuals received a "class status designation" according to the political, economic, and "moral" criteria derived from the Maoist categories. The "Reds" included workers, poor and middle-class peasants, party members, martyrs, and revolutionary intellectuals. The rest were "Bad": landowners, rich peasants, counter-

revolutionaries, outcasts, and enemies of the Party—this last designation could mean virtually anyone. These labels, which were transmissible from parents to children, illustrate Mao's intention to objectify to the utmost the contradictions of society. Until their disappearance during the de-Maoization process of the 1980s, these hardened categories brutally shaped the political, civic and material survival of every Chinese.

In 1954, although a new constitution had made China a "popular democracy" presided over by Mao, socialism was the order of the day. The Chinese Communist Party had won the Civil War with strategies and techniques developed at Yanan. By initiating mass collectivization, it would take on an even more formidable challenge. Conceived and carried through as an enterprise of domination, the transition to socialism would entail meeting the demands of the economy, in a poor country. The 1953 census revealed the staggering number of citizens, at a time when peace was creating a Chinese baby boom.

Would political success be transformed into economic and social prosperity? Would the coalition of Yanan survive ten years of an accelerated plunge into the abyss of the Great Leap Forward?

Strengthened by his victories, Mao Zedong threw himself into the struggle against under-development and inequality. In true imperial style, he sought to possess the minds and souls of his people. This new enterprise would meet with less success than the previous one, which had benefited from the impetus of war. The huge forces it harnessed announced what Maoism was to become: a permanent war against society and its institutions, and a police State.
Ph © Gamma

Chapter 6
EMPIRE IN **D**ISPUTE
19**55**–19**65**

TRANSFORMING POLITICAL VICTORY INTO ECONOMIC PROGRESS WAS THE GOAL OF THE GREAT LEAP FORWARD, THE "CHINESE WAY" TO SOCIALISM. BUT THE EXPERIMENT HAD DISASTROUS RESULTS. MAO, UNDER PRESSURE, WOULD TAKE THE STRUGGLE IN ANOTHER DIRECTION.

I n 1955 Mao decided to break with the industrial development and gradual collectivization outlined in the first Five Year Plan (1953–57). With his consummate tactical skill, focusing at times on the economic front, at times the political, Mao pushed allies both at the summit and at the base of the Party to apply his activist methods to the areas of production, management, distribution, and planning. The "Chinese Way" would lead Mao to redefine the very institutions of the socialist State: once, during the forced passage to communism during the Great Leap Forward (1958); then again, when the failure of the Great Leap had put Mao and his brand of despotism on the defensive with the very survival of the Revolution at stake.

The implementation of the Five-Year Plan created new elites and new forms of inequality. This was inevitable, for China had too many people and too few resources. Collectivization, not intended to effect the immediate redistribution of land, progressed gradually at first. In the countryside, the rhythm of collectivization was dependent upon that of industrial advances: in early 1955, only 13 percent of peasant households belonged to the "lesser" cooperatives, modest groupings of a dozen (or several dozen) families who retained ownership of the land, receiving compensation proportional to its yield. Mao had high hopes for the success of the Stalinist model (which his own "way" would take several steps further), but he quickly saw the constraints of applying it to the whole of China, which was vastly more diverse than Yanan. He

By setting out on the "Chinese Way" to socialism, Mao sought to realize the dream of the early revolutionaries: bring China up to its rightful level—in other words, catch up. In 1958, a vast public works campaign was begun. In contrast to the opinions of his predecessors, for whom economic progress was dependent upon opening China's markets, Mao judged that China should "rely on its own strength." In truth, this strength was mostly muscular; but for Mao, Chinese muscle was the real wealth of a nation that he compared to a "blank page" upon which he vowed to write "the most beautiful characters."
Ph © Roger Pic

The "Chinese Way" to socialism defined by Mao applied equally to city and countryside, where 90 percent of the population lived. But throughout the 1950s, it would favor rural China in practice. In contrast, the Cultural Revolution (1966–68) would be a mostly urban phenomenon. Here, Mao inspects collectivized farmland in 1955
Ph © Archives CDCC

delayed acting on his conclusions until 1955, perhaps because a more important affair was unfolding simultaneously. Gao Gang, a Communist official from Shaanxi risen through the Party ranks, had been Proconsul of Manchuria before heading the Commission for the Plan at Beijing. Intent on bringing prosperity to his Manchu fief, Gao Gang pushed for the first great projects of the Plan to be implemented there. Mao would not tolerate this. In his view public works had to be undertaken in the Chinese interior, with strict Party control ("tutelage") over the contractors. It is clear that Gao Gang was also seeking to reinforce his position at the head of an independent admini-stration—the Plan—overseeing the economy. Alongside this ambition, Gao had actually mounted a concerted offensive against the supreme directorate of the Party: Liu Shaoqi and Zhou Enlai. He also had possible ties with the Soviets. At any rate, Mao did not delay his counterattack, but carried it out in the wings, in order not to discredit his Party in the eyes of the people. Criticized in 1953, "deposed" in February 1954, Gao's condemnation hung in suspense until April 1955. Deng Xiaoping replaced him in the Politburo and at the Plan. The political situation was ripening for Mao's true convictions about progress to be expressed in action. But this was the last time he would defend the coalition of Yanan.

The High Tide of Socialism (1955–1956)

Another of Mao's signature phrases, the "high tide of socialism in the countryside" was the vast wave of collectivization that swept China in 1955–56. The political sphere was now bound to the economy by a special plan for agricultural development, distinct from the Five-year Plan. New, "superior" cooperatives (each comprising a hundred families) were supposed to harness a huge potential for mobilization and growth. The masses were put to work on roads, canals, land reclamation, and reforestation—the very opposite of

NEW ELITES, NEW INEQUALITIES

The first beneficiaries of Mao's industrial development policy were the cities. Adapted from the Soviet model, and implemented with their technical and logistical support, the Chinese Communists' Five-Year Plan sacrificed their historical ally, the peasantry. Indeed, it taxed their resources to the limit through the practice of requisitions without resulting in local investment. As the Party's hold on the countryside strengthened, and the transition to socialism moved forward, the Party no longer relied on the peasant masses, but instead on the new rural elite, the local militants and Party officials, and their peasant clienteles— a testament to the political and social mobility created by the Revolution. Mao would use this new "base" to great advantage until the Great Leap Forward. The rural elite's power was reinforced, to the detriment of traditional hierarchies, even within the family. By encouraging Party officials to outdo each other in their activist fervor, Maoist initiatives drove a wedge into local interests and the factions that appeared in the rural microcosm in spite of the political lockdown: a Party chief could in this way enhance his image vis-à-vis his superiors by vanquishing any number of rivals. In the cities, the regime also rested on its worker base, or at least on those workers lucky enough to be employed in large, state-owned factories, in contrast to the rest. Urban inequality was a general phenomenon; even before the elimination of the wealthy upper class (landowners and bosses)—still protected by the social, if not political, reality of the New Democracy—choices had been made in the transition to socialism. The needs of accelerated industrialization had attracted legions of unskilled workers to the cities, where they were hired on temporary contracts that denied them the social services provided by the Danwei. The Danwei system also created a dichotomy between, on the one hand, the large businesses and the Danwei (which disposed of huge funds allotted by the Plan), and, on the other, the majority of the businesses nationalized in 1955–56. Most of these were either too small or considered non-strategic (consumer goods, services, etc.), and for this reason received piecemeal allocations, hardly sufficient to provide housing, daycare, schools, or clinics for their workers.

A new movement of the masses toward socialism is about to get underway in the rural areas [...]. And yet, some of our comrades are shuffling along, like women with bound feet, complaining incessantly: "Oh, but you're going too fast!"

Mao Zedong, July 1955

the slow and costly strategy of industrial mechanization espoused by the Five-year Plan. Mao abandoned the idea of redistributing the modest surplus, instead increasing the surplus through mass labor. The "Small Leap Forward" as it was retrospectively dubbed, consisted in completely revisioning collectivization.

The Small Leap had great effects, not least of which was increased inequality. Industry and commerce were nationalized in the cities in 1956, creating an imbalance of entitlements in the traditional public sector and the heavy industries nationalized long before. The Party bureaucracy stepped up its involvement, provoking more dissatisfaction among businesses used to the looser climate of coalition times. Party officials were present in the workplace, overseeing discipline and the distribution of wages and bonuses, but the Party could do little to alleviate the housing crisis that struck the cities. The peasants had great difficulty identifying with these "superior cooperatives." They were being forced to trade a system of compensation based on input for fixed, egalitarian wages, and to leave cooperatives whose boundaries had been drawn along those of villages and coherent territories, for larger and more impersonal groupings. Party officials organized work and decided what to cultivate. The only reason why Maoist collectivization was still less dramatically felt than in Soviet Russia was because the Party had already penetrated peasant society to the core. In some areas, though, where resistance to the Party line was powerful enough, collectivization had to beat a calculated retreat.

The "high tide" of 1955 considerably perturbed the top Party apparatus. But developments in the USSR were to compound its effects. Initiated by Khrushchev in February 1956 (Stalin had died in 1953) the process of "de-Stalinization" sent a veritable shock wave through the Communist Party. According to the official line, Stalin had made mistakes, but he remained a great revolutionary. Mao's solitary exercise of power was reinterpreted in the light of the criticism of Stalin, reviving the call for sharing power.

For himself, Mao found the Party lacking in spirit and cohesion. If society as a whole was too self-indulgent in its dissatisfaction and too absorbed in local interests, it was the Party cadres' fault. A rectification campaign to integrate the changes of collectivization became the occasion for Mao to purge the Party. Intellectuals were rallied to join the criticism. Echoing a classical poem, Mao famously said, "Let 100 flowers bloom together; let 100 schools of thought contend."

One Hundred Flowers (1957)

This slogan had been coined by Zhou Enlai in early 1956 to revitalize an intelligentsia wrung dry by Party campaigns the year before. Mao Zedong appropriated the slogan to achieve his own ends, calling, in a decidedly un-Stalinist fashion for rigorous debate, transparency, and reconciliation. Hostility between Mao and other party leaders eased somewhat: a twelve-year plan was launched in April calling for "balanced industrial development" and the cooperative movement relaxed. Mao now took aim at

The Great Leap was preceded by the "Small Leap" of 1955–56. Mao took on inequality between the cities and countryside, and between social classes. Without renouncing planned industrial development, he sought to harness the huge physical and political potential of worker mobilization.
Ph © Roger Pic

Party apparatchiks, who had rallied behind Liu Shaoqi's reluctance to use rectification within the Party to send a message to society as a whole. In the fall of 1956, with de-Stalinization in full swing, the Eighth CCP Congress kept Mao at bay. His ideas were no longer considered the summit of Marxism-Leninism, and the post of general secretary, which Mao had neglected when he became President of the Central Committee, was re-established through the nomination of Deng Xiaoping. Mao's response was to return to the provincial base of the Party and defend Stalin, invoking rebellions in Poland and Hungary (Soviet tanks had entered Budapest in 1956, as they were to do in Czechoslovakia in 1968, during the Cultural Revolution). Contradictions seemed poised to split the Party. Would China itself fall apart, too?

Mao's opponents felt the Party's dominant position would be imperiled were it to break with the very effective consensual "work ethic." Mao replied that

society had sufficiently changed for these contradictions no longer to be antagonistic—they were weaknesses coming from within that needed rectification (or plain repression). His aim remained, above all, to seduce the masses at the Party base. His famous speech of February 12, 1957 on the "fair and just solution to the contradictions apparent in the Chinese people" announced the appli-cation of the Yanan political agenda to the whole of "socialist" China.

By the end of April, the intelligentsia was being called upon to overcome its fears, trumpet forth the new truths of 100 Flowers, and provide the ideological drumbeat of Mao's latest rectification. But as soon as reviews in the *Communist Youth* and organs of the other "democratic parties" began spurting out articles criticizing "Communist dictatorship," phase two of Mao's plan went into effect. On June 8, with Mao's benediction, the Party leadership proclaimed a "class war against right-wing deviants." In spite of its precise

"*F*inally, I am in the open sea!" (June 1956): at a time when his choices were being hotly contested within the Party, Mao, here with a group of writers, rejoices at being once again in a fighting stance. He spurred the intellectuals to an all-out assault on the Party, the Campaign of 100 Flowers (1957)—only to condemn several hundred thousand of them as "rightists" later on.
Ph © Roger Pic

The "Chinese Way" was born out of the first significant break with the USSR. The failure of Mao's 1957 encounter with Khrushchev (here, with Bulganin, in Moscow) foreshadowed the breakup that would come three years later. In 1955 at Bandung, Mao had already laid the foundations for non-alignment: "The Eastern wind is stronger than the Western Wind."
Ph © Archives CDCC

designation, the offensive was aimed not only at declared opponents to the regime, but at the intelligentsia itself, who were caught in Mao's diabolical trap! Subtly but insistently pinpointing the very essence of its role, Mao took direct aim at intellectual independence, denouncing "technicians, scientists, and researchers" who strayed from "socialist" knowledge. There had been precedents for this cruel treatment of the intelligentsia. The New Democracy, while accepting those whose skills legitimized a certain class prestige, was not overly warm to intellectuals in general.

The 100 Flowers turned out to be the eye of the cyclone that would bring in the Great Leap, itself the precursor of the Cultural Revolution. This moment of open debate, when contradictions were openly discussed for the first time in years, was like a carnivorous flower, ready to close upon its prey. In 1942, Mao had made wide cuts at the top of the Yananese intelligentsia in order to homogenize his revolution. In 1957, the operation was repeated at the national level, with the goal of homogenizing an entire socialist society. His strategy was to jump-start political and economic progress in China by gaining absolute control over the intelli-gentsia; the 100

Flowers campaign was the ideal shortcut. Moreover, it enabled his political comeback within the Party leadership.

From the vantage point of the West, familiar with the failures of Stalinism, these events might be perplexing. But Mao's conception of totalitarianism necessitated the massive adhesion of the intellectuals and the no less massive exploitation of their talents. Interestingly, though, the voices of protest that had risen up at Mao's instigation represented the "other" legacy of May 4th: a political movement that had never crystallized into institutional, authoritarian form, and whose possibilities of expression depended—as they still do today—on the weakness of the regime. At any rate, Mao's enterprise was facilitated by the rallying of the Communist Youth and students, such as Lin Xiling, who adopted Maoist exaltation and attempted to reconcile the Communist struggle with their democratic convictions. In spite of their concern, many intellectuals and politicians were taken in by the nature of their personal ties with the Chinese leader. These ties explain much of the murkiness of Communist China's relationship with its intelligentsia, and the success of the 100 Flowers campaign.

*M*ao Zedong was behind the development of the Chinese atomic bomb, celebrated here in a 1967 test. Ten years previously, he had brought back from Moscow a secret agreement and imposed the nuclear option on a Party leadership that would have been content with a traditional army supported by a modernized economy. Mao judged a nuclear arsenal to be a crucial complement to the popular militias mobilized by the Great Leap.
Ph © Roger Pic

From the Great Leap Forward (1958) to the "Dark Years" (1959–61)

By the end of 1957, Mao re-established his position in a unified Party. The timing was perfect, for the latest statistics confirmed what many feared: gains in agricultural production were too meager to boost investment in industry, which in turn couldn't supply enough jobs and resources to the cities. The demographic explosion, due to a long-delayed peace and improved sanitary conditions, cancelled out the increased national wealth. Individuals saw no gain in income or food rations. But anti-right-wing terror kept quiet, protestors who had come to the fore during the 100 Flowers campaign.

Rid of all significant opposition, Mao could now push the Great Leap. The Twelve-Year Plan rose from its ashes, and the cooperative movement was resuscitated as well. If 1957 served to avenge the insult of 1956, the next year confirmed Mao's immense power. During the winter of 1957–58, several provincial officials, in Henan for example, launched large-scale irrigation projects, putting "politics at the command post" and boasting "self-reliance"—in other words, not asking for Party funds, but resorting to requisitions instead. The magnitude of this mobilization led them to improvise new institutions, great communes (soon dubbed "People's Communes") that would receive Mao's blessing in August 1958.

The objectives of the Second Plan were revised upward, at the same time the central authorities in

THE PEOPLE'S COMMUNES (1958)

The People's Communes created an entirely new form of society. Families, houses and plots of land were abandoned by entire populations that the Party lodged by the thousands, or tens of thousands in collective dormitories, and nourished in immense refectories. Commune members were paid exclusively and equally in "work-points," whose value fluctuated according to the commune's performance and resources. Party brigades and teams (made up of the former, lesser and superior cooperatives) organized the work force, and distributed rations and points. Agricultural labor alternated with assignments to public works or to the factories. Political and military training was an essential component of the multi-tasking communes. For their role was not only to boost economic development, but also to raise militias—over 200,000,000 men in 1959, a huge army Mao could point to in his diatribes against the USA Development in Mao's conception consisted not only of urban and rural areas, industry and agriculture, but also, traversing the economic sphere as well as the political (the Stalinist, activist, mobilizing force of Maoist doctrine). The activist economy jettisoned compromise and sectorization in favor of the "white page," China's immense work force, that Mao Zedong thought was an inexhaustible source of progress —provided that it be driven with a clear purpose and an iron hand. Mao's goal was not only to advance public works, but also to produce more: in this respect the example of the steel industry is typical. Symbol of socialist production, smelting furnaces appeared all over the country amid great fanfare. In the cities, where communes were introduced only in 1959, production was reorganized before people. Factories and neighborhood authorities opened informal workshops for professional training, and intellectuals were xiafang (sent down) to the countryside to engage in manual labor. Concurrently, imports of industrial equipment skyrocketed. The cities swelled with the ranks of displaced peasant workers, a new urban proletariat. ■

charge of economic administration were shut down. The Great Leap Forward was affirmed as the "permanent revolution." The State was literally put to sleep on Mao's orders, in order for the voice of Chinese unity to obtain maximum resonance. The vocabulary of politics would henceforth be made up of the achievements of the people. This "moral" strength, in Mao's view, would give China the decisive impetus to catch up, not only with the West—achieving the old revolutionary dream of a shortcut to development—but also with the USSR. By showing that he was capable of creating a revolution within the revolution, Mao sent a challenge to Khrushchev's policy of peaceful and gradual progress to a communist society.

Indeed, the Great Leap was not quiet. In the summer of 1958, international tension was high following Mao's bombardment of Nationalist-held islands off the coast of Fujian. Production forecasts

In order to double steel production and overtake Great-Britain (then the third most powerful economy in the world), China built tens of thousands of improvised smelting furnaces. Production soared, but stocks of poor-quality steel remained unsold. Meanwhile, peasants were so exhausted by their new labor that they failed to bring in the harvest, provoking the famine of 1960–61. The lack of organization of the massive efforts undertaken, however, caused output to level off, having barely progressed since 1957.
Ph © Archives CDCC

were exaggerated with information falsified by Party underlings trying to fulfill quotas established by the leaders. A statistical mirage confirmed the expected miracle, in the absence of the statisticians and plan administrators themselves. An exceptional harvest reinforced collective enthusiasm. But as soon as autumn passed, the harsh reality revealed itself. The peasants, exhausted from their work in the forges, had neither the time nor the energy to bring in the harvest, which rotted in the fields. Steel produced in the rural forges turned out to be useless, after thousands of tons had been wrought into plow and kitchen utensils... Chaos and famine loomed.

Moreover, the requisitions from the country to the city continued unabated, with quotas based on the false results, not the real situation in the countryside. The Party was strangling the peasants. Mao heard the alert, though, and began reigning in his zealous troops (Chen Boda even wanted to abolish currency!). He announced an impending rectification in the communes, and decided to abandon the post of President of the People's Republic to Liu Shaoqi (December 1958–April 1959).

In the midst of this attempt to calm the political scene, Mao faced a challenge from within. Peng Duhuai's offensive at the Plenum of Lushan (July–August 1959, see sidebar) failed, but it was a poisoned victory for Mao. To all appearances, with Lin Biao having replaced Peng as Defense Minister, the circle had reformed. In reality, the complicity shown by the barons in the eviction of one of their own, and in the Great Leap, would inexorably lead them to rise up against Mao much as Peng had. But by then, they stood on a mountain of corpses: 15 to 30 million Chinese perished during the famine of 1959–60. The army repelled millions of peasants fleeing the communes. Millions of others, who had been drawn to the cities by the "boom" of 1958–59, were thrown out, along with countless intellectuals and officials. The

"**O**ne ladder is not enough, two brings you to the sky, but alas! Your efforts are in vain, Mr. Statistician." This popular song from Shanghai (1959) mocked the Great Leap and its excesses, aiming indirectly at Mao himself. Satire would be the favorite weapon of Mao's post-Great Leap opponents.
Ph © Archives CDCC

aftermath of Lushan was a great turning point. Why did the Chinese repeat the mistake of the Bolsheviks, not deposing a Mao at least as weak as Stalin was on the eve of the Great Terror? Were they afraid of Mao's threat of guerrilla-style opposition? Doubtful, for they would be skeptical even in 1966, when Mao ignited the Cultural Revolution under their noses. A lack of political imagination? Loyalty? Intense personal rivalries were silenced by Liu Shaoqi's ascension to the Presidency. Indeed, with Liu, Mao had brought a vast number of upheaval-weary apparatchiks back into his

PENG DEHUAI'S CHALLENGE

Although the Great Leap's failure elicited criticism as early as February 1959, Peng Dehuai's attack was more serious. An advocate of a classical military resting on a solid economic base, he rejected the Maoist line in its entirety. Just as he had denounced Mao's "frog-like mind" back in Jiangxi, he had no faith in the economic anarchy of the Great Leap, nor in the combination of the atom bomb and people's militias on which Mao based his national defense. Peng went further, openly accusing Mao of an abuse of power. Mao, aware since his duel with Wang Ming that feigned humility is the best defense, called for free discussion within the Party. He even invoked the illustrious example of mandarins of old who had dared to speak out against the reining authorities, such as Hai Rui during the Ming Dynasty (1515–1587), who was stripped of his position after sending a critical letter to the Imperial Throne. Either he or Zhou Enlai commissioned the historian Wu Han to write a narrative based on this story, with the following moral: dare to be Hai Rui, and the Emperor will share the kindness of his justice with him. Yet things did not turn out so well for Peng Dehuai. He attacked Mao and his leadership during the great summer gathering of the CCP at Lushan (Jiangxi Province) in July–August 1959. Mao himself had invited Peng to the congress, as if to diligently confront the clamor of criticism directed against the Great Leap. Mao turned the tables in his favor with his usual uncanny political intuition. Feigning to believe in a plot against him, he threatened to raise another Red Army. He also made a show of self-criticism, though attributing his mistakes to those of Marx and Lenin and summoning the Party to assume its share of responsibility. For militants and high-level officials, too, had compromised themselves in the Great Leap: "I have caused great chaos and I am responsible for it. Comrades, you must also analyze your

own responsibility…. It has cost us dearly, but we have released the winds of communism and given the people the chance to learn an important lesson." ∎

Peng Dehuai, Minister of Defense, had been Mao's arch-enemy since the thirties. It was he who suggested dethroning Maoism in 1956. Three years later, he spoke out against the Great Leap in no uncertain terms: "peasants are being forced to beat the gong with cucumbers… [we must] build socialism, not brag about it." Sacked in 1959, he was persecuted further during the Cultural Revolution. His rehabilitation in 1978 would signal the start of de-Maoization.
Ph © Archives CDCC

Among the "sacred" images of the "return to the source," this one, taken during the construction of a dam near Beijing in 1959, associates Mao Zedong with Peng Zhen, Mayor of China's capital city. In the early 1960s, Peng Zhen would spearhead the anti-Maoist revolt, becoming the first victim of honor of the Cultural Revolution. A survivor, he would be one of Deng Xiaoping's main partners at the head of the Party after Mao's death.
Ph © Archives CDCC

fold, while playing off the Liu camp against other pretenders, notably in the military. Finally, the crisis of Lushan took place at a time when China's aggressive policies were pushing it toward an isolationist stance. After Taiwan, the US, and India, Khrushchev seized Mao's economic failure to embark upon an anti-Beijing crusade. It is possible that Peng Duhuai may have planted the seeds of Moscow's turnaround; he had visited in the spring of 1959. The Soviet shadow, to which Gao Gang and Wang Ming owed their early demise, certainly left its mark on Peng.

Despot in Danger (1962–65)

The catastrophe of 1960–61 delayed the final phase of the conflict opposing Mao and the other Party leaders. Blame was laid on the weather, and on the retreat of Khrushchev's experts in summer 1960 (in reality the chaos of the Great Leap had sidelined Soviet assistance already in 1958). Discretely but surely, however, Liu Shaoqi, Deng Xiaoping, Chen Yun, Peng Zhen (Mayor of Beijing), and Zhou Enlai committed themselves to a "revisionist" course of action, which Mao would combat in open, unrepentant rebellion. The communes were abandoned in favor of work brigades and contracts with individual peasant households. Specialists and technicians once again had some say in running factories, and the economic administration of the Plan was re-established; some market mechanisms were reintroduced, as well as a hierarchy of salaries and bonuses. The first reforms of the post-Mao epoch would grow out of this early "readjustment."

While Chen Yun pushed for a tentative market presence, less heavy industry and accumulation, and more consumer activity—therefore more consumer goods—the leaders of the Plan won the day with Zhou Enlai's "four modernizations." This strategy, announced in 1964, emphasized a market-driven economy; the idea that the economy possessed its own laws independently of the class struggle and activist politics would unite the anti-Maoists until 1978, when Deng Xiaoping was finally able to implement their program. Already in 1962, Deng's conception was remarkably pragmatic: "It matters not if the cat is black or white, but whether it catches the mouse."

Things went south politically as soon as the famine of 1961–62 abated. In January 1962, an assembly of thousands of Party and State apparatchiks gathered to hear an official explanation of the disastrous results of the Great Leap. Liu attributed 70 percent blame to human error and 30 percent to natural factors; he held the Party and the people co-responsible. Peng Zhen, Mayor of Beijing, explicitly accused Mao: since 1961, the future victim of honor of the Cultural Revolution had regularly had satirical allusions to the Great Leap and to Mao's frivolous planning published in the Beijing press. Wu Han, author of the tailor-made, romantic version of *Hai Rui* (see Peng Dehuai sidebar), wrote a play, this time against the "bad emperor." A cartoon caricatured the famous monkey, Sun Wukong, a character in *Voyage to the West* (one of Mao's favorite novels), known for his readiness to launch assaults on the palaces of the heavens, but so oblivious

In 1959, the Tibetan rebellion was brutally repressed by Peng Dehuai, in whose eyes it represented a China ready to explode. The Communists had occupied Tibet, vassal to the Qing Dynasty since the early 18th century. Since 1959, there have been few incidents until recently; the regime has maintained a constant level of repression.
Ph © Wu Miao/Ana

of the consequences of his acts that the intervention of the Buddha himself is required.

Constrained by the gravity of the famine, Mao decided to opt for a war of words. In his poetry, he embroidered on the theme of the solitude of the one who is right before everyone else: "Let us acclaim today Sun [Yat-sen] the great sage, for evil thunderclouds are looming." He did not have long to keep his true thoughts in check. In 1962, China's situation had improved; in September, Mao launched an offensive against the medical profession in his latest "movement of socialist education." This new revolutionary struggle concerned the Party as much as society as a whole, with "revisionism" as the designated enemy. The break with the USSR in 1960 gave Mao an additional arena in which to deploy his rhetoric in diatribes against Khrushchev, and also against Tito, written by a brain trust of theoreticians of Maoist activism. Mao stopped short of the personal denunciations of revisionists that would herald the beginning of the Cultural Revolution.

To what extent was Mao's power truly threatened? Did the Party apparatus really wish the "socialist education movement" upon itself, or was it coerced? Whatever the answers to these questions, it is certain that Mao used the apparatus to consolidate perhaps

the only true victory of the Great Leap: the disciplined fusion of the Party—and the Chinese people—with Mao's ideology, his goals, and his person. This was not accomplished overnight, but through a sustained effort on several fronts.

Mao was successful in imposing his ideology, for his themes ended up carrying the day in the Party. Even his staunchest opponents had to take his allies seriously. The masses of mid-level officials had lost their enthusiasm, though. Following close upon the failures of the Great Leap, the contradictory signs from on high were the last straw. Local party authorities were prey to local interests and factionalism, and observed with increasing indifference the ideological quarrels and struggles for power at the summit of the Party hierarchy. This disenchantment would never abate; in fact, it was to develop at an increasing pace, inspiring post-Mao doctrines of decentralization and de-collectivization. Adherence to his dictates in the aftermath of the Great Leap was desultory at best: the Party base went through the motions of Maoist ritual.

The structure around which Mao had built his hopes was incarnated in the Dazhai brigade in Shanxi Province. The exceptional record of self-reliance of this unit was in large part due to the aid of the main bastion of Maoism: the army. Lin Biao had reorganized the armed forces along the lines of Yanan, complete with political re-education. Rank was abolished (in favor of collective rituals), and the dual thrust of a people's

From 1962 on, Jiang Qing took on an increasing importance at Mao's side, beside Chen Boda, his secretary and theoretician. Lin Biao's Army supported and staged Jiang's "revolutionary operas"—here, The Red Lantern—which spearheaded Mao's cultural offensive.
Ph © Roger Pic

An offshoot of the "socialist education movement," the Cultural Revolution started with intellectuals being sent to the countryside in 1964. This was a means to remedy a "form of degeneracy" that Mao had diagnosed before, in 1949: after the "sugar-coated bullets" of the bourgeoisie (i.e., corruption during the New Democracy), the "enemies without weapons," the revisionists, were now corrupting China's youth.
Ph © M. Riboud/Magnum

militia and nuclear weaponry re-emphasized.

In the cultural arena, a new genre appeared: the "revolutionary opera." The work of Jiang Qing, who had been rehabilitated, these elaborate dramas sent a message to the people that culture was to be the decisive battleground in the war between the "capitalist way" and the "proletarian way." The Cultural Revolution began in earnest in 1964. To be sure, the Party apparatus only followed to the extent of its own interests, doing its best to limit the scope and application of Mao's initiatives. Mao seemed to be pedaling in thin air, but he was far from out of the game. He had the army on his side—although not everyone loved Lin Biao—and a firm hold on international diplomacy. Zhou Enlai and Kang Sheng treated him with respect, pending more overt support for the Cultural Revolution, and Mao's own personal guard—a veritable parallel secret service and intelligence organization—kept him informed of everything. Mao's position was a complex one; he controlled key areas in all sectors, without totally controlling any one sector. He was simultaneously a clan chief in a system given over to factionalism, and the recognized supreme leader of the CCP.

This accumulation of influence betrayed a weakening of the regime. Although Mao was far from marginalized, his authority was diminished. Symbolic power was not something Mao would satisfy himself with for long, however. Liu Shaoqi interrupted him in a Politburo meeting in January 1965, and Deng Xiaoping suggested he not come back the next day. He did, with the Party constitution under his arm, from which he quoted the right of each member to express himself freely. Mao was getting worried; in his view the bourgeoisie was taking over. In addition, he imagined plots against his life. Khrushchev's overthrow in 1964 haunted him. In October 1965, he wondered aloud, before a public of local party officials, "Who will be the Chinese Brezhnev? What is to be done?"

The answer: revolt. In the end, Mao would overturn the Round Table and revive the Revolution, all the while keeping to the well-worn path of Yanan. Obstinacy and arrogance, however, would spur him to another revolutionary Leap. The qualities that had been his guardian angels during his rise to power were now his demons.

The Mao-Liu tandem—activist and apparatchik—was the political pivot of Maoism's triumph. Strained in 1955–57, their alliance bounced back during the Great Leap Forward (1958) and survived the Peng affair. It would not survive the "Dark Years," which broke the Yanan coalition, opposing henceforth pragmatists and Maoist activists.
Ph © Archives CDCC

Chapter 7
THE SHATTERED EMPIRE
19**66**–19**76**

IN 1966, MAO ZEDONG PROVOKED A POPULAR REBELLION IN ORDER TO REGAIN POWER. THE FAILURE OF THE CULTURAL REVOLUTION WOULD PAVE THE WAY FOR THE SUCCESS OF REFORMS UNDERTAKEN IN 1978 BY DENG XIAOPING.

T o offer his throne to the eternal Revolution would have been a fitting end for Mao. But Mao against the Party remained Mao the strategist of power: he attacked the power of others, not the Party. He was far from the romantic of his youth. The rebel wearing the uniform of the People's Liberation Army and the armband of the Red Guards was a caricature of his own contradictions. Plotting and maneuvers supplanted great designs, the thirst for order was stronger than the thirst for rebellion; popular participation led to generalized violence. Faced with chaos, the supreme leader effected a brutal about-face. Mao's great work would disintegrate into terminal factionalism, for which his death proved the only cure. Like an old man locked up in silence after a youth of tumult, the re-conquered empire was a broken one.

Once again, Mao's initial tactic in the fight against the Party took the form of a trap, disguised as an invitation to revolt. Until the student uprising of May 1966, it was through the factions that Mao progressed in his penetration of the political institutions. The first to fall were Peng Zhen and the leadership of the Ministry of Culture. In November 1965, Mao had a denunciation of Wu Han's *Hai Rui* published in Shanghai, where he had his winter quarters. Peng, president of the voluntarily inactive group put in charge of launching the Cultural Revolution in 1964, seized the case, thereby deviating the force of the blow. Wu Han was exonerated in February 1966: he wasn't looking for political trouble, his mis-

The troops in Mao's 1966 assault on the Party apparatus were recruited in the schools and universities, called upon to "remake" the Revolution. The Red Guards would answer his call with an extremist zeal; they were responsible for numerous incidents of brutality, and the bloody repression that followed in 1967–8. If divinity were measured by the enthusiasm of the masses, then Mao Zedong had surely become a god.
Ph © Roger Pic

The first flames of the Cultural Revolution licked schools and universities in the spring of 1966 with stifling rules and pitiless academic selection. Students easily accepted an elitist administration that kept political files on every one of them with the Party, and responded enthusiastically to Mao's incendiary encouragement.
Ph © Roger Pic

takes had been academic, etc... Mao bit back at these "Theses of February." On May 16th before the Politburo, he pronounced them void, ordered the destitution of Peng Zhen, designated a new group to coordinate revolutionary activity (Chen Boda, Jiang Qing, and Yao Wenyuan), and denounced the infiltration of the Party leadership by capitalists. A second trap was being set.

The Return of the Rebel (1966)

On May 25th, a female professor at Beijing University posted a *dazibao* (political manifesto) aimed at the Rector's elitist policies, poor results, and "foreign science." There soon followed other attacks against academism, "bourgeois" knowledge, and its supporters. Campuses reached the boiling point with Mao's blessing of the Beida *dazibao*; the press was brought in to call upon Chinese youth to "crush the monsters and demons" like Sun Wukong, the monkey of legend. In much the same way that Jiang Qing had enticed Yao Wenyuan to take up the trumpet of criticism in November 1965, the *dazibao* of May 25th was inspired by the wife of Kang Sheng, who (though hesitant at first) rallied behind Mao's offense in February. These early maneuvers sum up well the double nature of the Cultural Revolution: on the one hand, enthusiastic rebellions against a society fossilized by rigid hierarchies; on the other, the struggle for power and factional cynicism. Mao praised the purity and energy of youth, just like Chen Duxiu had many years before. But the resemblance stopped there: the offensive of May–June 1969 had nothing to do with social harmony. It announced, all to the contrary, the Red Guard offensive of July 1969: a brutal, disorderly act of political terror. The Red Guard itself would fall prey to violence between hostile factions.

The Party leaders were gravely concerned by the reigning chaos. Liu Shaoqi consulted with the President: shouldn't Mao send out work brigades? Did he think Mao would content himself with factional revenge (the elimination of Peng Zhen) and letting off

THE RED GUARDS

Mao called on "the leaders of tomorrow" to harden their character in concrete struggle, "making" the Revolution. The only type of education that interested him now was political; an experience founded in each individual's violent confron-tation with authority. The personal cult around Mao, that magnified every step of his rise to power, triggered "struggle meetings" that rivaled those of the agrarian reform for their violence. Unmasking "capitalists" within the power structure, stigmatizing the escapees of the old order and the black sheep of the new, the Red Guards accused professors, landowners, and "rightists." These and other enemies of the People's Republic were pulled out of their jail cells or hunted down, forced to confess to imaginary wrongdoings, and punished

ten, twenty, a hundred times, beaten and broken. Mao's personal enemies—Liu Shaoqi and Peng Dehuai—were prime victims, the former dying in 1969, the latter in 1974. Some were enemies protected by anti-Maoist factions, like Deng Xiaoping in the South; Li Lisan however was executed in 1967. Class status regained vital importance: this was an indication of how far-reaching the onslaught. Intellectuals, the "ninth malodorous category," were relegated to the most humiliating tasks, and many of the innumerable works of China's artistic heritage—temples, statues, paintings, books—were marked for destruction. Schools, libraries, and museums closed for indefinite periods. From city to city, province to province, the Great Educator swept away all "old things." Pilgrims from the provinces gathered in Beijing

for huge, fanatical demon-strations to Mao's glory, in the hopes of receiving his personal blessing. Tiananmen Square became the stage of a Red Nuremberg. On August 18, 1966, the Great Sun, Great Educator, Great Leader, Supreme Commander, the "Bronze Emperor" as André Malraux dubbed him, appeared at dawn, before a throng of adorers, waving his *Little Red Book*. From August to November 1966, a human tidal wave submerged the capital and disorganized the transportation network. Zhou Enlai and his functionaries won points for his future by his diligent handling of the crisis. ■

some activist steam? Whatever the details of this internal debate, Mao's imperial and sibylline reply of "maybe, maybe not" was followed nevertheless by the apparatus moving into action with customary efficiency. Back in Beijing on July 18th, Mao had only to denounce a "plot against the masses," throwing more oil onto the fires of agitation. He took to wearing the Red Guard armband, and wrote his own *dazibao* during a Politburo

A re-education session. *"Reactionary elements" perform acts of self-criticism, while a Red Guard intones the lesson. On the wall, in large characters, a Maoist slogan: "Defend the Center." To the left, a quote from Mao: "All the reactionary things that you do not attack will not fall down by themselves. It's just like sweeping. If you don't use a broom..."*
Ph © Archives CDCC

meeting—"Fire on headquarters!"—and, in August, produced the charter of the Great Proletarian Cultural Revolution, under the slogan "We are right to rebel." Meanwhile, Liu Shaoqi (the "Chinese Khrushchev") and Deng Xiaoping—the "number two leader who follows capitalism"—were demoted, and Lin Biao promoted to second-in-command.

The rampage of the Red Guards during the summer disorganized the country, but left the Party intact. Exploiting rivalries within the movement, the authorities set up their own cells; people whose parents were Party officials used their "class status" to protect themselves.

This was when Mao decided to go one step further.

He gave his Red Guards the order to "take power" by relying on the workers. But the workers, who were to be used as a lever against the authorities, reacted according to ancient dividing lines. Foremen and other skilled workers were loyal to the authorities, while unskilled day laborers sided with the rebellion. When the Party and factory administrators upped the ante economically, the radicals raised the political

stakes by promising to abolish contracts and class status. In January 1967, the radicals of Shanghai, controlling a city that was in the grip of the biggest strike in its history, proclaimed a "Paris Commune"—which Beijing immediately refused to recognize. Officially, although the class struggle was now "installed" in the Party and the State, the apparatus as a whole could not be considered "antagonistically" infected. The groups or cells organizing the takeover, the Revolutionary Committees, were composed of revolutionary rebels, re-educated militants and Party members, and military personnel. The PLA was thrown into the fray, ostensibly to give a semblance of order to operations, while supporting "the left." But

Elements of the Black Gang accused at a "struggle meeting." The long bonnet is a reminder of those worn by landowners at similar meetings during the agrarian reform (1946–50). In his 1927 Report on an Investigation of the Peasant Movement in Hunan Mao praised the peasants for having imagined this excellent means of inversing the power relationship.
Ph © Archives CDCC

犬馬之労

The Cultural Revolution targeted the return of the bourgeoisie in the form of individuals and Party leaders—here, Liu Shaqi, Deng Xiaoping, and Peng Zhen. Liu Shaoqi died of poor treatment in 1969, one year after his exclusion from the Party as a "traitor" and "renegade." In 1967, Jiang Qing had searched the police archives of the city of Mukden (later Shenyang), obtaining proof that Liu had been arrested and released by the Guomindang in 1927. Actually, Mao himself had been through a similar experience with the Hunan police.
Ph © Archives CDCC

which "left"? Lin Biao's intense indoctrination campaigns had not been sufficient to homogenize the Army; commanders of provincial battalions (the only ones engaged) had an unfortunate tendency to join forces with local authorities, with whom they were well acquainted. These alliances were contested within the PLA, which was soon caught up in the whirlpool of factional strife. Above all, the Red Guards, whose radicalism was hardened by experience, vowed to stamp out, by force if necessary, the defectors.

With insurrections in the countryside spinning out of control, Zhou Enlai and his ministers were under siege in Beijing, in spite of Mao's promised protection. Attempts at arbitration by representatives of the center—itself split into two camps—had little hope of success. In July, the commander of the Wuhan garrison declared a rebellion. In August, the British Embassy was sacked. China could be said to be in a state of civil war, were it not for the even greater chaos that made the notion of war irrelevant. Like the Emperor's nightmare in *Water Margin*, Mao saw too the specter of an evil rebellion, illegitimate in that its victims were not only bad politicians, but the Empire itself. The time for reaction had arrived.

The Emperor Strikes Back (1967–68)

The Cultural Revolution's brutal brand of political activism fared no better than the equally brutal economic measures attempted. Mao hesitated for once at the edge of the abyss. Since his order to "suspect and criticize everyone and everything" did not include himself, he was exempted from the collective paranoia, and could afford not to insist too heavily. What he was defending was the difference that appeared in early 1967 between the version of Maoist activism that was institutionalized, and a current of anarcho-Maoism, which was threatening power itself. At this point, the form of organization embodied in the Party structure was truly Mao's life's work. It had begun with his embracing communism, then the Guomindang, continued with the experiments of Jiangxi and Yanan, and culminated in the Great Leap Forward—the work of his life. He was not about to see it destroyed by forces beyond his control. It would take a year for him to achieve a state of order. In a chaotic and brutal manner, he purged (summer 1967) the groups at the head of the Cultural Revolution of far-left elements. In October, the first of the Red Guards were sent to the countryside, and schools reopened. But the road was not easy. Revolutionary committees implemented what amounted to martial rule; factions vied for influence and numerous "leftist rebellions" broke out. But those revolutionaries who remained faithful to the ideals of 1966 prevailed; by the summer of 1968, they had managed to quell most of the unrest in the country. The Beijing campus was vigorously "rectified," and the

In January 1967, Maoist activists and Party officials fought over the Shanghai labor base. The victory of the former led to the creation of a Commune, along the lines of the Paris Commune of 1871. But Mao did not accept this mutinous form of power. The movement that he had instigated, undermined from the start by internecine conflicts, failed in the arena of power and social struggle.
Ph © Archives CDCC

rivers of southern China carried the victims of the Red Guards' savage terror campaigns out to sea. Hong Kong, however, swarmed with refugees fleeing peasant militias, heavy artillery and napalm. By the end of 1968, re-pression had begun to include "preventive" deportations: henceforth, year after year, until Mao's death, the regime would levy its tribute of young men and women fresh out of high school or college, and send them to "harden" in the fields. This trauma was experienced by an entire generation of Chinese. Rejected by the peasants who considered them useless—more mouths to feed—many led a miserable existence, torn between the hope of returning to the city and the despair of a humiliated faith.

Mao's Cultural Revolution could be compared to the

When Party officials from the North took control of the South in the 1940s, Hua Guofeng was put in charge of Shaoshan and Xiangtan: this luck saved his career. After crushing the Hunanese anarcho-Maoists, he was called to Beijing, when conflict broke out between Mao and Zhou on the one hand and Lin Biao on the other (1970–71). Head of the Secret Police, he was to become the pillar on which Mao's last edifice of political terror rested—and Mao's own designated successor.
Ph © Archives CDCC

French Revolution with its first, open stage, and later its terror. Neither a despot worn out by power nor a twisted tyrant, its instigator was a solid block of contradictions. His ideological fervor kindled the fires of discontent felt by the population vis-à-vis the established order embodied in the regime, and constantly harked back to the rebel tradition of early 20th-century China. The Cultural Revolution was an occasion to reconnect with values of heroism and personal sacrifice, lived out through confrontations with power and the class struggle.

It was also a social crisis that allowed Mao to exploit popular tensions to achieve his goals. He was no longer writing on a white page, as he enjoyed saying during the Great Leap—the peasants and Party officials, after the intellectuals, had had enough of ideology—but utilizing the broken ideals of those left behind, when the winds of social mobility had died down, in a society just as stalled as its politics. As factions began to crystallize in the early sixties, the transition to socialism produced its own inertia, with closed cities, an industry producing few skilled jobs or leading to dead-end careers. In contrast, the lucky few hoarded promotions and privileges of all kinds: at school, in the workplace, and in their administrative and political status.

The pragmatists, by insisting on the inevitable and irremediable nature of the social problems caused by the failure of the Great Leap Forward, gave Mao a clear advantage in winning over a significant portion of disaffected urban citizens to the idea of an authentic social movement: a revolution within socialism. But this last avatar of the Chinese leader's revolutionary vision was doomed as an impossible artifice. For how can revolution be held and nourished by a totalitarian system?

Mao's wish was not simply to reign over the

Revolution, he wanted to reign by Revolution. The crucial difference, which also defined its limitations, was in his believing in the possible complementarity between institutional and activist politics; in other words, in a resolution of his founding dilemma, one that he had inherited from earlier traditions, with both political and fundamentally Chinese attributes. The first revolutionaries had already addressed the question: Was it social dynamics, or political hegemony that drove the engine of history? Marx maintained the ambiguity; Lenin erased it: in his view, institutionalized political authority was capable of crossing "objective hurdles." From the twenties, Mao adapted this belief in the form he gave—along with many others of his generation—to voluntarism.

Yet Mao's path in Chinese history revived Marxist ambiguity. Not with respect to social dynamics—for his rural policies pointed out the instabilities and inertias inherent in Chinese rural society—but with respect precisely to what was supposed to be society's prime arena of expression: a political space created by the authorities. The Yanan politicians were supposed to embody the reconciliation of the militant and the Party official, and by that token the resolution

Mao called young people "Guardians of the Revolution," but said they had disappointed him in 1968—when they stopped blindly following orders from the central authorities. It was soon their turn to be "rectified" by the soldiers, workers, and above all by the peasants. "Young graduates" were sent en masse to the countryside from 1968 on: the military-style departure ceremonies hid the reality of an exile that many went through suffering great despair and anger.
Ph © Roger Pic

of the dilemma inherited from their precursors. But Maoism in practice consisted in a total reorganization of Chinese society according to the rules and criteria of communist totalitarianism, in spite of mass participation through mobilization campaigns. This duality proved highly efficient during the period of the Communists' rise to power, from 1936 to 1964. It was less suited to the demands of economic development and the rigidity of the socialist system. Mao leaned more and more toward tyranny as the faith of his followers became less spontaneous. As the Cultural Revolution skidded out of control, he spun about between the two poles of his political philosophy, breaking the Round Table of the Yanan coalition and squandering the enthusiasm of Party officials and the people's trust that had made him the largely accepted Emperor of a China rehabilitated in all its glory in the 1950s. The Cultural Revolution's brand of totalitarianism was a marriage between rebellion and absolute power that was bound to be discovered false in the end, a monstrous ransom paid for the dream of total activism, a dream of emancipation that worried too little about limiting the powers of the liberators. Mao, son of a certain Chinese democratic ideal, proved ad absurdum the delusional nature of this ideal. He murdered the Chinese dream of a perfect democracy. Independently of the detours taken or not taken and the differences between this and other totalitarian regimes, failure was at the end of the road, and the final and definitive divorce of Mao's ill-fated coupling of revolution and absolute power. As cruel as it was, this was not a lesson that Mao had intended to inflict on his people. They learned it themselves, through the pain of their own experience.

The Rupture (1969–76)
Mao's last years, the "decade of calamity"

MAO ZEDONG: A POSTMODERN FAUST?

In 1981, Deng Xiaoping succeeded, in negotiations with the right wing of the post-Mao regime, in obtaining a compromise. Mao's legacy was officially judged "70 percent good, 30 percent bad," with attenuating circumstances: Mao had made mistakes, but had sought to serve the Revolution. According to the Resolution of June 1981, it was "the tragedy of his situation." The word "romantic" came up often. Isolated in his determination to continue the Revolution, Mao ended up being seen as a fallen rebel. The Cultural Revolution unfolded as an accelerated, "B-movie" version of his entire political career: soldier, rebel, activist, more emperor than ever, demi-god— all coexisted in one impotent despot in a fractured country, a country that rejected him, a country short of utopias. Mao had successively alienated intellectuals, peasants, the Party, the young, and the workers. No one was left to follow him, except a brigade of pretenders (each more ultra-Maoist than the next, such as the blindly loyal Hua Guofeng or the brutal fanatic, Jiang Qing) who held him hostage to their their own ambitions. Mao himself cultivated this climate of conspiracy and rebellion.

Edward Snow, who met him in 1970, when the challenge from Lin Biao suggested steering away from excesses (like the personality cult), drew the conclusion that Mao saw himself as a vagabond wandering with his umbrella. But behind the image of the outlaw without religion, loomed the Emperor, whose laws reached as high as the sky. He made it clear that he definitely did not romanticize failure. There was in fact no "pre–1949" as opposed to a "post–1949" epoch, a time of innocence in the struggle, followed by the frustrations and excesses of power. Though Mao constantly exerted his conqueror's will to the utmost of its capability, he was not, in contrast to Hitler, bound up in the "all or nothing" logic of collective self-destruction. His hold on power was due to his awareness of the relative strengths and relationships between the forces of the political arena, and the brilliant tactical skills he had displayed in factional conflicts and at war—his instincts led him also to compromise when necessary. It was a combination of suppleness and single-mindedness that made his mix of constructive and destructive political actions so original,

and so enduring, for retreat was always temporary, and the struggle could always be renewed. Mao's beliefs in the eternal return of Revolution, and in its gradual perfectibility, were firmly grounded in his own experience. After the failed Republic, came May 4th; after Shanghai, the Jinggangshan; after the debacle of Jiangxi, the Long March and Yanan; after the disaster of the Great Leap Forward, the first Cultural Revolution. He had no qualms about announcing further revolutions, in order for the mixed results and ensuing criticisms to further the cause of the New Humanity freeing itself from the chains of History. His final silence was no more an abdication than it was a sign of disappointment. Mao delegated his ambitions, and Maoism waged an endless war against a society that it was no longer in the process of transforming. This Mao recalls Goethe's second Faust, a blind old man, stubbornly trying to make the sea go backwards after his workers have fled; the singing he hears behind him is that of the demons digging his grave. For Mao, there would be no redemption. ■

The circle of the faithful is no more: after Liu Shaoqi (background), Lin Biao, Mao's closest companion at arms, died according to the official version, when the plane in which he was escaping after having tried to assassinate Mao crashed in Outer Mongolia. According to another hypothesis, Jiang Qing, or Mao himself, had him executed. Moscow recently confirmed the presence of his body in the wreckage of the plane, but Mongolian authorities continue to deny this.
Ph © New China Pictures/Magnum

(1966–76), have yet to be fully assessed. One thing is certain: factional strife had wrought destruction far beyond the Party apparatus. Massacres among the civilian population had caused the rivers of the South to run red once again, and added to the already swollen contingent of refugees in Hong Kong (which provided proof of the massacres). And elsewhere? The worst was probably not the maelstrom of 1966–68, but the heavy undertow that followed until 1976, an oppressive round of parades, robotic political rituals, and real violence that further paralyzed the Party and destabilized society. The explanation of this paradox— the continuation of a political movement in a country condemned to running in place socially and economically—lies in the strength of factional tensions. Behind the empty political rituals, the base—local officials and the population— retreated into their daily preoccupations and problems, which were far from being solved.

Mao Zedong thus left behind a kind of fallow jungle, with a few successes: an agricultural revolution, less "red" than "green," in the sense that technology was improved, with rural factories reconverted to produce fertilizer; medical care too attained a respectable level thanks to the penetration of Party organization throughout the countryside. But China remained perversely underdeveloped: industry was strong, but produced useless goods. The countryside groaned under the sheer weight of the human population, and the cities were leveled, divided into regimented neighborhoods, considerably diminishing their productive energies. Demographic pressure, slow promotion in most careers, slow economy: the official, impersonal though egalitarian Party line did nothing to alleviate these ills, nor did it regulate the competition of individuals and clans for material gain.

In this China of blocked perspectives, a variety of survival strategies proliferated. Clientelism, connections, black markets, corruption, and other criminal activity all flourished in a climate of poisonous rivalries and organized political revenge embodied in the famous "cam-paigns." On paper, Mao had achieved his "activist" goal of an energized, politicized, and homogenized Chinese people; in reality, exploiters and victims lived side by side, in a fragmented, apathetic society. At the top of the pyramid, ongoing factional strife was evidence of the decadent state of politics. Lin Biao, in 1969 consecrated second-in-command in the highly militarized Chinese State,

Mao and the successor he didn't choose: Deng Xiaoping. A moderate Maoist until the post-Leap era, he survived because of protectors in the South. He was placed in power by Zhou Enlai, overriding opposition from ultra-Maoists led by Jiang Qing, and Mao's own preference for Hua Guofeng—to whom he allegedly said, before dying, "With you in charge, I go reassured."
Ph © New China Pictures/Magnum

disappeared mysteriously in November 1971, between the secret visit of Henry Kissinger in July and the much-publicized one of President Nixon (February 1972). He had opposed a rapprochement with the US to counter Soviet threats, as he had the reconstitution of the Party machine carried out by Zhou Enlai with Mao's blessing. Although the disastrous errors of the Great Leap Forward were not repeated in the countryside, and birth control was finally addressed, the "realist" side of Mao had not taken precedence. He encouraged the attacks led by the ultra-Maoists (Jiang Qing and the other Shanghai leaders: Yao Wenyuan, Wang Hongwen, and Zhang Chunqiao, with whom Mao would form the "Gang of Four") against the Prime Minister's policies, such as rehabilitating Deng Xiaoping (1973), and returning, in 1973, to the Four Modernizations of 1964. But Mao's appearances and public declar-ations became rarified, and he took on the air of an automaton. With Zhou Enlai ill with cancer, and Deng Xiaoping keeper of the pragmatist flame, the war between the two wings of the Party was waged less subtly than ever, under the expectant eye of the police and the generals. Aside from a few localized outbreaks in 1975, the extremists had great difficulty arousing the sympathies of an exhausted people, who hoped for nothing more than a "reasonable" succession to Mao. This option was embodied in the Prime Minister and his men, not in the ultra-Maoists.

The succession would in all likelihood have been more direct if death had not taken Zhou Enlai first (January 8, 1976). When the ultras joined forces with Hua Guofeng's police to evict Deng Xiaoping, the people's disappointment and incitements to revolt were such that thousands converged on Tiananmen

Spontaneous posting of dazibao in Beijing, near Tiananmen Square in November 1978. In the middle, the large characters read: "We must re-evaluate Mao (30 percent bad, 70 percent good)." Another reads: "Democracy. Human Rights." Deng Xiaoping used the discontent manifested in the street against Hua Guofeng and the neo-Maoists. After his victory, Deng would muzzle the more radical of them, including Wei Jingsheng, who advocated a "Fifth Modernization": democracy.
Ph © Archives CDCC

Square on April 4th, provoking a bloody onslaught by the police. Deng Xiaoping once again took refuge in the South, becoming in absentia the pragmatists' successor-in-waiting. With Mao's death on September 9th, and other events that seem to accompany the fall of an emperor—the death also of Zhu De, dean of Mao's Long March companions, and an earthquake in Tangshan—the ultras' offensive encountered a wide resistance. The Four were arrested by the police on October 6th, and the last pockets of loyalist resistance were brought under control during the winter. When Deng took power, he proclaimed a return

1989

to the Four Modernizations. With Mao's body laid in state next to Zhou's, Hua Guofeng still aimed to save the body of Maoist doctrine. All he had, though, was the old loyalist guard—generals and politicians implicated, as he was, in the April 1976 massacre at Tiananmen—and the inertia of the party officials. Deng Xiaoping quickly secured the support of the Party base, by emphasizing the advantages that would accrue from future reforms. He indicated the way by directing against Hua Guifeng the resentment of the numerous victims of Maoism, spurred on by the intellectual fervor of 1978. The general aspiration to tranquility and prosperity, allowed Deng, once he had eliminated Hua and negotiated a controlled de-Maoization (1978–1981), to implement reforms that would change the face of China, without abolishing the Communist regime.

China after Mao

The platform of Dengism consisted in pacifying China, healing its wounds, and putting it back in the saddle internationally. For the economy to take off, the political system had to be streamlined, and a pact of non-aggression concluded with society, in the form of a watered-down capitalism. Although Deng did not provide any avenue of political expression outside the Party, the Chinese people celebrated their liberation, in spite of the ever-present authoritarian implications. Initial success was due most of all to competent teamwork and a coherent program, both of which were embodied in the "historic" anti-Maoist guard. These men gathered together; putting aside differences concerning the right amount of reform and the timetable of de-Maoization, and implemented the decisive return of the peasants to family-based landownership, abolished the People's Communes, and opened up the national economy. Although private enterprise and

Tiananmen, April 1989: as with the death of Zhou Enlai in 1976, the passing of a leader in whom the people had high hopes—Hu Yaobang, nominated to the supreme party post by Deng Xiaoping in 1981—crystallized popular resentment in a movement spearheaded by students. Beyond the circumstances and the contradictions of the movement, the symbol that remains is that of the June 4th repression immortalized in this scene—that of a regime that, in spite of Deng's adjustments, relied above all on brute force.
Ph © S. Franklin/Magnum

Since 1989, Mao's embellished image has become a nostalgic reference for a disoriented society. People remember stable prices, privileges for workers, the honesty of Party officials, and most of all the glory of a "liberated" China, and associate Mao Zedong with Zhou Enlai, the "Good Prime Minister."

free markets were allowed and the power of technocrats restored, the framework of a socialist industry remained untouched. Thanks to his political versatility, Deng Xiaoping was able to impose his reforms through alliances with conservatives as well as reformers. Both had to come to terms with Deng's refusal of systematic solutions; beneath Deng's apparent openness and efforts to decentralize, the bureaucracy was essentially untouched—and corrupt practices on the part of Party officials were largely tolerated.

While this balancing act proved its efficacy in healing conflicts inherited from the Mao era, Deng had more difficulty when his own measures began creating new areas of tension. Geographic rivalry reappeared with the reemergence of "Blue" China's coastal regions, especially in the South, causing runaway inflation in a burgeoning economy. Tension increased between the bureaucratized cities and the newly prosperous neo-capitalist periphery; it was further exacerbated by the bureaucrats' own growing interest in getting a piece of the action, in a society where money had suddenly become all-important.

Dissatisfaction in Chinese society found echoes in a new student movement, and in the emergence within the Party of a generation of politicians more radically committed to reform. They advocated the generalization of a market economy and private property—and democracy—going beyond the scope of a transition out of Maoism. This widespread desire to change society completely came to an ill-fated climax in the spring of 1989, although Deng had already separated from the reformists in 1987–88. The conservative reaction ended in 1992, and economic reforms resumed.

China bounced back, first of all because of the economic dynamic created by the reforms, but also because of the retreat of ideology in a State now much more devoted to management and money-making. It could afford to do so: thanks to efficient State repression, division within the post-Tiananmen social movements, and the stiff realities of post-Communism. The intelligentsia revised its democratic hopes downward. The "Deng System," which ended with the demise of its namesake, died less decrepit than Maoism, but without having resolved its conflicts. Deng's successors, torn between technocratic and authoritarian tendencies and the desired evolution of institutions, have opted for a strategy of "re-centering" and "adjusting" of a reformed China.

As a criticism of Deng Xiaoping, this tack illustrates the transitory character of his regime. The changes that he facilitated are rooted deep in China, in the double revolution to which Deng devoted his life. The imperial agricultural empire of old, catapulted into modernity in the space of a half-century, had also been deeply transformed by totalitarian communism, to such a point, in fact, that Deng's own reforms precipitated his decline. For a long time, the tumult of revolution had blocked or delayed modernization; now, "Blue" China was beating the rhythm, and draining masses of peasants from the countryside to the urban and coastal areas. This tendency was slower but irreversible, constituting a break with the past even more radical than Maoism, or the reforms of the post-Mao epoch. The end of Deng's generation, tamed and betrayed, would erase the final effects of their

1989: Portraits of Mao in Tiananmen Square. While the people carrying them are clearly dissatisfied with the unpopular Deng Xiaoping, they failed to launch a political movement. This was certainly the main weakness of Deng's and the "Red Capitalists'" adversaries: they tried in vain to resuscitate Maoism as a political doctrine, despite Mao's own last, posthumous defeat.
Ph © P. Zachmann/Magnum

undertaking. They symbolized the end of the old China, for they were part of a tradition—as had been their enemies—that no longer held currency. Thence the climate of fear and uncertainty surrounding the succession of Deng. When Mao died, China awaited the succession with hope. Now people revived his image and the good side of Maoism (price stability, honest Party officials, China's greatness), forgetting the image of the revolutionary and the despot, or associating those qualities with Zhou Enlai. Such a phenomenon cannot be explained simply by nationalism or power maneuvers, for it is a sign, one among others, of the state of the Chinese soul today. Neither pitiless capitalism nor the "normalized" Deng regime, nor Nationalist propaganda, can capture the dreams of a highly diverse society, with its different strata having come out of the Communist experiment with highly divergent conclusions.

When, with a more and more complete integration with the rest of the world, China might serenely and with confidence open up to itself—its individuals, its interests, its ideas, its religions constantly held in check by official governments and ideologies—then all these human concerns might be addressed openly; no longer for economic convenience, but because of their own importance and value. That would be democracy. But Chinese democracy is only one of a number of much less promising scenarios for the future. The frustrations and aspirations that make democracy so urgent will not soon dispose of the means to bring it into being. Even Taiwan has a way to go on its road to freedom, and it is only an island!

The half-smile, benevolent and polite, that one often sees throughout the vast People's Republic today, could well be one of irony, a wink toward its Achilles' heel: somewhere, between the sphere of private interests and beliefs, no longer fused with those of the traditional family, and the political sphere of post-Deng China, something is missing. There is a place, which Emperors, Confucius, and Mao occupied. Empty, it waits.

Chronology

1736–1796/99	Qianlong's (Kan Tsung) reign
1842	The Treaty of Nanking ends the First Opium War
1857–1860	Second Opium War
1851–64	Taiping Rebellion
26 Dec. 1893	Mao Zedong is born at Shaoshan, Xiangtan District (Hunan Province)
	Treaty of Shimonoseki sanctions Japan's victory over Russia
1895	The Reformists in power for 100 days
1898	Boxer Rebellion
1900	Governmental reforms; rise of revolutionary activity
1901–1911	Imperial exams abolished; Sun Yat-sen forms the Sworn League
1912	Chinese Republic; foundation of the Guomindang
1913	Failure of the parliamentary regime; dictatorship of Yuan Shikai
1916	Death of Yuan Shikai; chaos amid the rule of warlords
4 May 1919	Patriotic and intellectual effervescence
July 1921	Foundation of the Chinese Communist Party in Shanghai
1923	First United Front CCP–Guomindang; dictatorship of Yuan Shikai
1925	Movement of May 30th; Mao Zedong is a rural agitator
1926–28	Expedition of the North against the warlords
1927	Rupture of the United Front; Chiang Kai-shek rules in Nanking
End 1927	Armed insurrections; flight to the Jinggangshan Mountains
1930	Failure of Li Lisan's bid for power; Mao dominates the guerrillas at Jiangxi
1932–1933	Mao superceded in Jiangxi by Zhou Enlai and Wang Ming
1934–1935	Long March, conference of Zun'yi; Zhang Guotao's defeat
December 1936	Incident at Xi'an; Chiang Kai-shek accepts union
1937	Japanese invasion; Second United Front
1938	Wang Ming defeated, Mao Zedong heads the CCP at Yanan
1945–1946	Rupture of the Second United Front; agrarian reform
1st Oct. 1949	Proclamation of the People's Republic of China
1955	Mao steps up collectivization
1957	The 100 Flowers Campaign; anti-rightist movement
1958	Great Leap Forward; tensions with the US and the USSR
1959–1961	The "dark years" of economic collapse and famine; Peng Dehuai's challenge; break with the USSR
1961–1965	"Readjustment" undertaken by Liu Shaoqi, Deng Xiaoping, and Chen Yun
1962–65	Conflict between "the Two Lines" (Maoists/Pragmatists)
1966–68	The Cultural Revolution unleashes chaos
1971	Elimination of Lin Biao; rapprochement with the US
1976	Deaths of Zhou Enlai and Mao Zedong; fall of the Gang of Four
1978	Deng Xiaoping in power; economic and political reforms known as "de-Maoization"
1985–89	An overheated economy fuels expressions of popular discontent
1989	Defeat of the reformist movement (Tiananmen Square)
1992	New series of economic reforms under Deng Xiaoping
1997	The UK hands Hong Kong over to China; Deng Xiaoping dies in February, succeeded by Jiang Zemin
2003	Hu Jintao becomes President

Brief Biographies

Cai Hesen (Tsai Hosen, Hunan, 1890–1931)—Mao Zedong's friend from Changsha, one of the first to discover communism in France.

Chen Duxiu (Tu-Hsiu, Anhui, 1879–1942)—an Occidentalist during the May 4th Movement, he became a prominent leader in the CCP (1921–1927).

Chen Yun (Jiangsu, 1900–1996)–member of the CCP leadership since the thirties, he supported, against Mao, then Deng Xiaoping, a moderately planned economy.

Chiang Kai-shek (Jiang Jeshi, Zhejiang, 1887–1975)—successor of Sun Yat-sen, chief of the Guomindang Party and of the Nationalist regime.

Deng Xiaoping (Teng Hsiao-ping, Sichuan, 1904–1997) —a faithful Maoist until the Great Leap Forward, then Mao's pragmatic successor after 1978.

Hua Guofeng (Shanxi, 1920–1981)—Guardian of the temple at Xiangtan, head of security at Mao's death, and Mao's designated successor; eliminated in 1981.

Jiang Qing (Chiang Ching, Shandong, 1914–1991)— Married Mao during the Yanan epoch, directed the Cultural Revolution, opposed Zhou Enlai and Deng after the fall of Lin Biao; arrested in 1976 with the rest of the Gang of Four.

Kang Sheng (Shandong, 1899–1975)—powerful head of the secret police, supporter of Mao and Jiang Qing against the party apparatus.

Li Lisan (Hunan, 1899–1967)—union leader who moved to CCP leadership. Mao's adversary in 1930, Li Lisan was executed during the Cultural Revolution.

Lin Biao (Lin Piao, Hubei, 1907–1971)—faithful to Mao since Jiangxi, he defied Mao in the aftermath of the Cultural Revolution in 1970 and disappeared in mysterious circumstances.

Liu Shaoqi (Liu Shao Chi, Hunan, 1898–1969)—an urban communist, he was Mao's alter ego from Yanan until the Great Leap.

Peng Dehuai (Peng Te Huai, Hunan, 1898–1974)—led the Red Army after Zhu De, and defied Mao in Jiangxi and in 1959, during the Great Leap.

Qu Qiubai (Chu Chu-pai, Jiangsu, 1899–1935)— theoretician of the United Front, successor of Party head Chen Duxiu (August 1927).

Sun Yat-sen (Sun Zhongshan, Guangdong, 1866–1925)—republican revolutionary, President of the Republic (1912), founder of the Guomindang.

Tan Yankai (Tan Yen-kai, Zhejiang, 1879–1930)— Hunanese warlord, Guomindang chief of Canton and Wuhan—and Mao's mentor in the 1920s.

Wang Ming (Anhui, 1905–1974)—head of the internationalists (the 28 Bolsheviks), Wang Ming challenged Mao in 1938 and later, from Moscow, during the Cultural Revolution.

Zhang Guotao (Chang Kuo-tao, Jiangxi, 1897–1979)— entered CCP leadership in the 1920s, and opposed Mao in 1935, after Zunyi.

Zhou Enlai (Chou Enlai, Jiangsu, 1898–1976)—like Zhang Guotao a CCP leader since the 1920s, Zhou who opposed Mao at Jiangxi, joined him again at Zunyi, became Prime Minister after 1949. During and after the Cultural Revolution, he held China together more than Mao himself.

Zhu De (Chu Te, Sichuan, 1866–1976)—leader of the Red Army at Jiangxi and at Yanan, faded from prominence after 1949.

Bibliographical Index

The Chinese Transcription

The *pinyin* system used by Beijing has spread little by little since the near-universal acknowledgement of the People's Republic and its "opening" to the world. Simpler than its predecessors (for example, it almost always avoids apostrophes), it can also be just as disconcerting, if not on occasion more so. Thus, what used to be "Peking" is now "Beijing." The "j" is pronounced "t" followed by a "ch" sound, which was approximately rendered by the "k" in Peking. In this book we have retained some of the more familiar usages (Nanking, Canton), as well as the dialectal pronounciations that have become habit (Chiang Kai-shek, instead of Jiang Jieshi in pinyin, which follows the pronounciation of the North of China). The reader should get used to recognizing Guomindang (as what was Kuomintang), Mao Zedong (instead of Mao Tse-tung), and Zhou Enlai (Chou En-lai), etc.